BHAKTI POETRY OF INDIA

An Anthology

For a complete list of our publications
go to the back of this book

BHAKTI POETRY OF INDIA

An Anthology

Translations, Introductions

PAUL SMITH

NEW HUMANITY BOOKS

BOOK HEAVEN
Booksellers & Publishers

www.newhumanitybooksbookheaven.com

NEW HUMANITY BOOKS

BOOK HEAVEN
(Booksellers & Publishers for 40 years)
47 Main Road
Campbells Creek Victoria 3451
Australia

ISBN: 978-1490969831

Indian Poetry/Spirituality/Bhakti/Indian Religion/Bhakti/
Indian Studies/Indian Literature/Indian History

CONTENTS

Bhakti & the *Bhakti* Poets of India... page 7

The Main Forms in the *Bhakti* Poetry of India... 16

THE POETS...

Appar 23, Andal 31, Jayadeva 39, Janabai 52, Namdev 60,

Dnaneshwar 70, Lalla Ded 81, Vidyapati 92, Chandidas 102,

Kabir 112, Nanak 138, Surdas 149, Mira Bai 159, Tulsidas 171,

Eknath 183, Dadu 192, Rasakhan 200, Tukaram 209,

Ramdas 218, Bahina Bai 226.

"To penetrate into the essence of all being and significance

and to release the fragrance of that inner attainment

for the guidance and benefit of others,

by expressing in the world of forms,

truth, love, purity and beauty...

this is the only game which has any

intrinsic and absolute

worth.

All other, happenings, incidents and attainments can,

in themselves, have no lasting importance."

Meher Baba (Huma)

Bhakti & the Bhakti Poets of India

Bhakti is the love felt by the worshipper towards the personal God. It can be used in either the tradition of Hindu monotheism, Shaivaism or Vaishnavism. While *bhakti* as designating a religious path is already a central concept in the *Bhagavad Gita,* it rises to importance in the medieval history of Hinduism, where the *Bhakti Movement* saw a rapid growth of *bhakti* beginning in Southern India with the Vaisnava Alvars (6th-9th century CE) and Saiva Nayanars (5th-10th century CE), who spread *bhakti* poetry and devotion throughout India by the 12th-18th century CE. The *Bhagavata* · *Purana* is a text associated with the *bhakti* movement.

The *Bhakti* movement reached North India in the Delhi Sultanate and throughout the Mughal era it contributed significantly to the characteristics of Hinduism as the religion of the general population under the rule of a Muslim elite. After their encounter with the expanding Islam religion, *bhakti* proponents, who were traditionally called 'saints,' encouraged · individuals to seek personal union with the divine. Its influence also spread to other religions during this period and became an integral aspect of Hindu culture and society in the modern era.

'Devotion' as an English translation for *bhakti* doesn't fully convey two important aspects of *bhakti*... the sense of participation that is central to the relationship between the devotee and God and the intense feeling that is more typically associated with the word 'love'. An advaitic interpretation of *bhakti* goes beyond 'devotion' to the realization of union with the essential nature of reality as *ananda,* or divine bliss. *Bhakti* is sometimes used in the broader sense of reverence toward a deity or teacher.

Scholarly consensus sees *bhakti* as a post-Vedic movement that developed primarily during the era of Indian epic poetry. The *Bhagavad Gita* is the first text to explicitly use the word '*bhakti*' to designate a religious path, using it as a term for one of three possible religious approaches.

The *Bhakti Movement* was a rapid growth of *bhakti* beginning in Tamil Nadu in Southern India with the Saiva Nayanars (4th-10th century CE) and the Vaisnava Alvars (3rd-9th century... such as the female saint Andal... see her section following) who spread *bhakti* poetry and devotion throughout India by the 12th to the 18th century. The Alvars ('those immersed in God') were Vaishnava poet-saints who wandered from temple to temple singing the praises of Vishnu.

Like the Alvars the Saiva Nayanar poets softened the distinctions of caste and gender. The *Tirumurai,* a compilation

8

of hymns by sixty-three Nayanar poets, is still of great importance in South India. Hymns by three of the most prominent poets, Appar (7th century CE... see his poems following), Campantar (7th century) and Cuntarar (9th century), were compiled into the *Tevaram*, the first volumes of the *Tirumurai*. The poets' itinerant lifestyle helped create temple and pilgrimage sites and spread devotion to Shiva.

By the 12th to 18th centuries, the *bhakti* movement had spread to all regions and languages of India. *Bhakti* poetry and attitudes began to color many aspects of Hindu culture, religious and secular, and became an integral part of Indian society. Prominent *bhakti* poets such as Kabir wrote against the hierarchy of caste. It extended its influence to Sufism, Sikhism, Christianity and Jainism. *Bhakti* offered the possibility of religious experience by anyone, anywhere, at any • time.

Bhakti in the *Bhagavad Gita* offered an alternative to two • dominant practices of religion at the time: the isolation of the *sannyasin* and the practice of religious ritual.

In the twelfth chapter of the *Bhagavad Gita* by Vyasa Krishna describes *bhakti* as a path to the highest spiritual attainments:

Arjuna asked: 'My Lord! Which are the better devotees who

worship You, those who try to know You as a Personal God, or those who worship You as Impersonal and Indestructible?'

Lord Shri Krishna replied: 'Those who keep their minds fixed on Me, who worship Me always with unwavering faith and concentration; are the best.

'Those who worship Me as the Indestructible, the Undefinable, the Omnipresent, the Unthinkable, the Primeval, the Immutable and the Eternal;

'Subduing their senses, viewing all conditions of life with the same eye, and working for the welfare of all beings, assuredly they come to Me.

'Who fix attention on the Absolute and Impersonal encounter greater hardships, for it is difficult for those who possess a body to realize Me as without one.

'Truly, those who surrender their actions to Me, who muse on Me, worship Me and meditate on Me alone, with no thought save of Me,

'O Arjuna! I rescue them from the ocean of life and death, for their minds are fixed on Me.

'Then let your mind cling only to Me, let your intellect abide in Me; and without doubt you shall live hereafter in Me alone.

'But if you cannot fix your mind firmly on Me, then, My beloved friend, try to do so by constant practice.

'And if you are not strong enough to practice concentration, then devote yourself to My service, do all your acts for My sake, and you shall still attain the goal.

'And if you are too weak even for this, then seek refuge in union with Me, and with perfect self-control renounce the fruit of your action.

'Knowledge is superior to blind action, meditation to mere knowledge, renunciation of the fruit of action to meditation, and where there is renunciation peace will follow.

'He who is incapable of hatred towards any being, who is kind and compassionate, free from selfishness, without pride, equable in pleasure and in pain, and forgiving,

'Always contented, self-centred, self-controlled, resolute, with mind and reason dedicated to Me, such a devotee of Mine is My beloved.

'He who does not harm the world, and whom the world cannot harm, who is not carried away by any impulse of joy, anger or fear, such a one is My beloved.

'He who expects nothing, who is pure, watchful, indifferent, •
unruffled, and who renounces all initiative, such a one is
My beloved.

'He who is beyond joy and hate, who neither laments nor
desires, to whom good and evil fortunes are the same, such a

one is My beloved.

'He to whom friend and foe are alike, who welcomes equally honour and dishonour, heat and cold, pleasure and pain, who is enamoured of nothing,

'Who is indifferent to praise and censure, who enjoys silence, who is contented with every fate, who has no fixed abode, who is steadfast in mind, and filled with devotion, such a one is My beloved.

'Truly those who love the spiritual wisdom as I have taught, whose faith never fails, and who concentrate their whole nature on Me, they indeed are My most beloved.'

Thus, in the Holy Book the Bhagavad Gita, one of the Upanishads, in the Science of the Supreme Spirit, in the Art of Self-Knowledge, in the colloquy between the Divine Lord Shri Krishna and the Prince Arjuna, stands the twelfth chapter, entitled: Bhakti-Yoga or the Path of Love.

Shandilya and Narada produced two important *Bhakti* texts, the *Shandilya Bhakti Sutra* and *Narada Bhakti Sutra*. They define devotion, emphasize its importance and superiority, and classify its forms.

In Valmiki's *Ramayana,* Rama describes the path as ninefold:

Such pure devotion is expressed in nine ways.

First is association with love-intoxicated devotees.

Second to develop a taste for hearing My nectar-like stories.

The third is service to the Guru.

Fourth is to sing My kirtan (communal chorus).

Fifth is Japa or repetition of My Holy name and chanting My bhajans.

To follow scriptural injunctions always, to practice control of the senses, nobility of character and selfless service, these are expressions of the sixth mode of bhakti.

Seeing Me manifested everywhere in this world and worshipping My saints more than myself is the seventh mode of bhakti.

To find no fault with anyone and to be contented with one's lot is the eighth mode of bhakti.

Unreserved surrender with total faith in my strength is the ninth and highest stage.

Anyone who practices one of these nine modes of My bhakti pleases Me most and reaches Me without fail.

The *Bhagavata Purana* teaches nine similar facets of *bhakti*.

During the 14th–17th centuries, a great *bhakti* movement swept through central and northern India, initiated by a loosely associated group of teachers or saints. Ramananda, Ravidas, Srimanta Sankardeva, Chaitanya Mahaprabhu,

Vallabhacharya, Surdas, Mira Bai, Kabir, Tulsidas, Namdev, Dnyaneshwar, Tukaram and other mystics and poets spearheaded the *bhakti* movement in the North while Annamacharya, Bhadrachala Ramadas, Tyagaraja among others propagated *bhakti* in the South.

They taught that people could cast aside the heavy burdens of ritual and caste, and the subtle complexities of philosophy, and simply express their overwhelming love for God. This period was also characterized by a spate of devotional literature in vernacular prose and poetry in the ethnic languages of the various Indian states or provinces.

Beyond the confines of such formal schools and movements, however, the development of *bhakti* as a major form of Hindu practice has left an indelible stamp on the faith.

Philosophical speculation was of concern to the elite, and even the great Advaitist scholar Adi Shankaracharya, when questioned as to the way to God, said that chanting the name of the Lord was essential. The philosophical schools changed the way people thought, but *bhakti* was immediately accessible to all, calling to the instinctive emotion of love and redirecting it to the highest pursuit of God and self-realization.

Of course *bhakti's* message of tolerance and love was not often heeded by those ensconced in the societal construct of caste. Altogether, *bhakti* resulted in a mass of devotional literature, music and art that has enriched the world and given India renewed spiritual impetus, one eschewing unnecessary ritual and artificial social boundaries.

Sources...

Wikipedia article.
Bhagavad Gita: The Gospel of Lord Shri Krishna by Vyasa, Revised into Modern English by Paul Smith from the original translation by Shri Purohit Swami, New Humanity Books, 2012.
Bhakti Poetry in Medieval India: Its Inception, Cultural Encounter And Impact by Neeti M. Sadavangani, Sarup & Sons, New Delhi, 2004.

The Main Forms in the *Bhakti* Poetry of India

The Sloka

The *sloka* is the oldest form of rhyming poetry in India and was created by India's first great Sanskrit poet, Valmiki who composed the *Ramayana* (the story of Avatar Rama) and appears in it and lived around 3500 B.C. This method of using different rhyming couplets with each line having 16 syllables to create and epic poem and tell a story of a great soul was two thousand years later carried on by India's second great spiritual epic poet, Vyasa... the creator of the *Mahabharata,* the story of another Divine incarnation, the Avatar Krishna. Vyasa also appears in his massive work. Of course this is a precursor to the rhyming couplets *masnavi* poems of Persia of Firdausi, Rumi, Nizami, Sana'i and many others and those of Amir Khosrau in India.

The Vakh

The *Vakh* (like the *Sakhs* of Kabir... are four line (or two couplets) poems... in the form of a-b-a-b of 'sayings' that were mainly famous from the poems of the great female Sufi/Shaiva saint Lalla Ded, the 14th century Kashmiri poet

The Doha

Dohas are self-contained strict-rhyming couplets popular with the poet-saints of India like Baba Farid, Kabir, Surdas, Tukaram and many others. One has to be concise and insightful.

The Abhang

The *Abhang* is a form of devotional poetry sung in praise of Vitthala (Krishna as a child) also known as Vithoba. The same rhyme runs through the whole poem that is usually sung. Abhangs were first sung by the Varkari saints like Namdev, Janabai, Dyaneshwar and Tukaram in their native language, Marathi (see their sections to follow). These saint/poets sought to put the emphasis back on devotion and love towards God, in contrast to blind obedience of rituals and arcane religious practices. Many of the *abhangs* are devoted to the God Vitthal but many were criticism over the social injustice of that time. They were powerful preachings, useful even today

The Bhajan

The term *'Bhajan'* broadly means devotional song sung with or without music for the Lord. The lyrics of the *bhajan* constitute of praises for the virtues of the Supreme power, of philosophical teachings, of dialogues from ancient scriptures and spiritual literature. It is the most familiar form of doing *bhakti* – worship, in Indian tradition and is prevalent across the country. Covering all dimensions of the country, bhajans form the core of the devotional expression and are an indelible part of the social culture of India. It is a way of connecting an individual or a group to the Lord and even to the true meaning of life. Sung in different forms like *kirtan,* mantra chants and often woven in the musical notes, *bhajans* are the most beautiful way of expressing joy and gratitude.

Dialogues from scriptures and *Vedas,* and famous teachings of saints are often blended with Classical or folk music forms to form these devotional songs. As a practice these are sung in *satsangs* – gathering of people to listen to knowledge and perform prayers. *Bhajans* are considered to be intoxicating and alleviates the mood of the people.

All the states of India have their flavors of *bhajan* and are reckoned with devotees who composed them. Mirabai from

Rajasthan, Kabir from North India, Tulsidas from Uttar Pradesh and Surdas are renowned *bhajan* composers and play a significant role in Indian philosophy and devotional literature. A part of Indian culture, *bhajans* are known to one and all, from children to the elderly and are sung to unite the mind and the soul.

BHAKTI POETRY OF INDIA

An Anthology

APPAR (7th century. C.E.). Appar ('Father') was Saivite Tamil poet-saint, one of the most prominent of the sixty-three Nayanars. He was an older contemporary of another famous poet/saint Sambandar. His birth-name was Marulneekkiyar: he was called 'Appar' by Sambandar.

Appar composed 4900 poems/hymns of ten or eleven stanzas each, but only 3130 are available today. These are collected into the *Tirumurai* along with the compositions of Sundarar and Sambandar, Appar having his own volumes, called *Tevaram*.

Details of Appar's life are found in his own poems. His sister, Thilagavathiar, was betrothed to a military commander who died in action. When his sister was about to end her life, he pleaded with her not to leave him alone. She decided to lead an aesthetic life and bring up her only brother.

He is supposed to have stayed many years at Atikai with his sister before visiting other Siva temples to sing in praise of Siva. He heard of Sambandar and went to Sirkali to meet him and he and Appar travelled together singing hymns. Appar is said to have traveled to about a hundred and twenty-five temples in different cities or villages in Tamil Nadu. He is said to have attained Mukti (Union with God) at Tiru Pukalur Siva temple at the age of 81.

His poems involved glorifying the feats of Shiva in a particular location. The emotional intensity of the poems/hymns represent a spontaneous expression of thought as an emotional responses to God, the essence of *bhakti*. "Appar personifies Siva *Bhakti*, devotion to Siva, the ever auspicious God." R. Nagaswamy.

Further Reading...

Siva Bhakti by R. Nagaswamy, South Asia Books, 1989.
Appar: Tamil Poet, G. Vanmikanathan, Sahitya Akademi, Delhi, 1996.
Mysticism and metaphysics in Saiva Siddhanta: A study of the concept of self in the Sivajñanabodham of Meykanda Deva in relation to the mystical experience of Appar by J.X. Muthupackiam, Intercultural Publications, 2001.
Saint Appar (Shri Vâgisha Deva). by Pillai (J.M. Nallasvami) Foreword by P. Râmanâthan. Meykandan Press, Madras, 1910.
Appar Devarathil Vazhviyalum Iraiyeyalum (Tamil Edition) by A. Nalanggilli, Nabu Press, 2011.

From the Tevaram

You as ether and other elements are standing, praise be!
You have me as Your slave, never releasing... praise be!
You are lying concealed within as the spring, praise be!
You are sound of Word going on speaking... praise be!
As pure energy You there go on abiding... praise be!
Six Angas, four Vedas You were becoming, praise be!
As wind, You everywhere are pervading... praise be!
O Lord of Mount Kailas, praise be, praise be!

With spirits You love to dance in commotion, praise be!
O Lord Who snaps cycle of transmigration... praise be!
You delight in pulling all of our strings anon, praise be!
You pervade my bosom in such loving union, praise be!
You smote all the false ones in every town... praise be!
You abide in this breast, never to be gone... praise be!
You have the serpent around waist, upon... praise be!
O Lord of Mount Kailas, praise be, praise be!

You the triple, hostile towns were destroying, praise be!
You this heart in loving union were entering, praise be!
You, taking on this form, me were creating... praise be!
You my inner life... it in Yours was veiling, praise be!
O You Divinity that is all Skill practicing, praise be!
O One, Who the whole nation is hailing... praise be!
O circling cloud that goes on moving... praise be!
O Lord of Mount Kailas, praise be, praise be!

O Nectar that by the Devas is hailed... praise be!
You, Who this heart of mine entered... praise be!
Lord of divine form Who flaws removed, praise be!
You rose up straight as fire that blazed, praise be!
O Clarity, that honey has conferred... praise be!
You stand as God of gods, undisputed, praise be!
You dance in the fire of the cremated, praise be!
O Lord of Mount Kailas, praise be, praise be!

You are the World of many towns, villages, praise be!
You rose straight as fire that has no edges, praise be!
You pervade everywhere in form of Flames, praise be!
You are in my heart, always having access, praise be!
You are lives in water and their shadows… praise be!
You are beyond compare in Your Oneness, praise be!
You are cloud that is dark to great excess, praise be!
O Lord of Mount Kailas, praise be, praise be!

You came in many, one Form becoming… praise be!
O God that even the gods aren't knowing, praise be!
You all the grass with life were investing, praise be!
You entered my heart, never to be parting, praise be!
As manifested lives You all are pervading, praise be!
You hold the world… it are not forsaking, praise be!
You are fire, the life of stone, its striking, praise be!
O Lord of Mount Kailas, praise be, praise be!

You are music, our melodic mode is You, praise be!
You annul sins of who contemplate You, praise be!
You became numbers, letters, words too, praise be!
Lord, Who leaving my heart will not do, praise be!
You, Who became ether, earth, fire too, praise be!
You Who higher than highest is You... praise be!
You, Who are the pupil of the eye too, praise be!
O Lord of Mount Kailas, praise be, praise be!

You don't blink, You aren't breathing: praise be!
God, Who from my heart isn't going; praise be!
You Parvati in Your body are sharing, praise be!
You Who the seven aeons are being... praise be!
Who ate poison one can't be eating... praise be!
O Aadi, first, perfect One, abiding praise be!
You are Flame that is all-forgiving, praise be!
O Lord of Mount Kailas, praise be, praise be!

You do not age, aren't born, never dead: praise be!

You, Who before Beginning manifested, praise be!

O God of all gods, hailed by every god... praise be!

You move... everywhere have pervaded, praise be!

O yes! You are my all, O my Beloved... praise be!

I grieve, by many troubles overwhelmed, praise be!

You save me, O my mountain of gold... praise be!

O Lord of Mount Kailas, praise be, praise be!

You are the extensive space supporting all, praise be!

You are the length and the breadth of all... praise be!

Your feet and crown to all were invisible, praise be!

There, You abide, and are unknowable... praise be!

You kicked to death cruel Death for all, praise be!

You stay as shrine in my heart to recall, praise be!

You are thunder, lightning in the pall, praise be!

O Lord of Mount Kailas, praise be, praise be!

You are not eating and are not sleeping, praise be!

You know Vedas without even reading, praise be!

Your toe Lanka's king was crushing... praise be,

and then You him in joy was gracing; praise be!

To music, words, You were listening, praise be!

Long ago my heart You were entering, praise be!

You are Eye of the world All-seeing, praise be!

O Lord of Mount Kailas, praise be, praise be!

ANDAL (approx. 8th century A.D.) Andal who was one of the twelve Alwars (immersed in God) and a female saint, lived in the first half of 8th century A.D. She was born as Godai at Srivilliputhur near Madurai. Her father found her while tending the garden and brought her up as an adopted child. She grew up in holy surroundings, worshipping the Deity and listening to holy discourses, Vedas, Epics, Bhajans, etc. From childhood onwards she listened to the *leelas* (pranks) of Krishna with rapt attention and developed a deep love for the Lord.

Andal helped her father in weaving flower garlands to offer to the temple Deity every day. One morning her father Perialwar observed her wearing and adorning herself with the flower-garland intended for the Deity and herself looking into a mirror and enjoying it. He considered this as an act of sacrilege and with great anguish failed to offer the garland to the Deity on that day. The Lord appeared in his dream and informed him that He relished only the garland worn by Godai and that in future flower garlands worn by Godai alone be offered to Him. From then she was called 'Andal' (one who ruled Bhagwan). It became a routine for Andal to wear the flower garland prior to offering to the Deity. As Andal grew up her love for Krishna also increased and she resolved to marry Him.

Andal imagined herself as a *gopi* at the time of Sri Krishna, collecting all girls at Ayarpadi at dawn during the Margali month, day after day performing the ritual on the banks of the river Yamuna and bathing the Deity. This procedure, expressed lucidly in thirty poems/songs in Sanskrit is the topic of *Tiruppavai*. Andal also sung 143 poems in which her expression of intense love to Krishna, in varying moods of bridal love... tender hope, utter dejection, joyful triumph, woeful sorrow and surrender, in *Nachiyar Tirumozhi*. She is said to have eventually merged with the Lord.

Further Reading...

Antal and Her Path of Love: Poems of a Woman Saint of South India, Translated by Vidya Dehejia, State University of New York Press, 1990.

Concepts of Sri Andal's Tiruppaval, by Chenni Padmanabhan, R.P. Publications, 1995.

Minstrels of God, Part One, by Bankey Behari, Bharatiya Vidya Bhavan, Bombay, 1956. (pages 118-25).

The Great Integrators: The Saint-Singers of India by Dr. V. Raghavan, Ministry of Information & Broadcasting New Delhi, 1964. (Pages 117-8).

Thiruppavai: With an English Rendering, by Antal, Translated by Ramaswamy D. Iyengar, Teacher's Publishing House, Madras, 1946.

Hymns of the Alvars, by J.S.M. Hooper, The Association Press, Calcutta, 1929. (Pages 49-58).

Consider Our Vow: An English Translation of Tiruppavai and Tiruvempavai by Norman Cutler, Muthu Patippakam, Madurai, 1979.

The Poems of Ancient Tamil, by George L. Hart, University of California Press, Berkeley, 1975.

The Poems of Andal (Tiruppavai & Nacciyar Tirumachi) Translated by P.S. Sundaram. Ananthacharya Indological Research Institute, Bombay, 1987.

The Secret Garland, Antal's Tiruppavai and Nacciyar Tirumoli, Translated with Introduction and Commentary by Archana Venkatesan, Oxford University Press, 2010.

From Tiruppavai

Listen to our idea of coming to You...
in the small hours of the morning, do!
we will bow to Your lotus-feet, blue:
You, born with the cowherders, too!
You should not leave not accepting
our service, O Lord, it is something
not just for today and then leaving:
for all time, to You we're belonging!
Because we'll You alone be serving:
all other desires aside be sweeping!

In this, the auspicious month of January,
this day with the light of moon to see...
come bathe, O maidens, rich, of Aypadi,
maidens in homes of those cowherders...
He with sharp spear Who kills His foes
without mercy, the son of Nandagopa,
He... who is the darling son of Yasodha,
Who wore garlands and is a young lion,
dark, small red eyes, face like the moon:

Lord Narayana, with drum us sway...

we bathe, all hail our Goddess Pavai!*

*Note: Tiruppavai belongs to the Pavai genre of songs, a unique Tamil
tradition sung in the context of the Pavai vow observed throughout the
month of Margazhi (January), originally by unmarried girls praying to the
Pavai goddess (related to Parvati) for a blissful married life.

Listen, who in this world live joyfully

to deeds we must do to live truthfully,

and sing of Him, the Supreme Lord...

Who, sleeps upon that snake, hooded

within sea of milk, at dawn bathing...

no *ghee* nor milk we will be consuming:

we won't with kohl eyes be painting...

and flowers our hair won't be adorning.

We will do no unfit deeds and we will

not speak evil words, give alms we will!

And, we will be joyful along the way...

as we walk: all hail our Goddess Pavai!

As we in name of that One, bathe, sing,

Who the whole world covers... we bring

to our mind all our vows and three rains

each month upon land falls that explains
good conditions as fishes leap in the tall
rice paddies and into the buds of lilies fall
the sleepy bees and the full udders of our
cows will flood bowls with milk... as our
fingers press udders and wealth this day
will be ours: all hail our Goddess Pavai!

Lord of rain, deep as sea, give everything...
dive into the depth and Yourself be filling;
then rise with Your body black becoming...
like the form of that One in the Beginning.
Flashing like disc in hand of Padmanabha,
that One of broad-shoulders, O so fairer!
Your thunder like His conch-shell roaring,
rain on earth... from *saranga* bow, pelting.
May we all prosper who bathe in Margali
waters today: all hail our Goddess Parvai!

When purified we come, flowers strewing,
with songs on our lips that One adoring...
in our hearts, upon that One meditating,
Krishna, of northern Mathura, praising...

of the sacred stream of Jamuna, the ruler,

and the shining lamp of every cowherder;

Damodaran, Who brightly lit the womb

of His mother, put mistakes in the tomb

like cotton that in the fire will burn away

into the dust: all hail our Goddess Parvai!

Listen, birds are singing, are you hearing,

hearing the silver conch's deep sounding

in the shrine of Lord of the Garuda bird?

O child, now get up... haven't you heard?

Sages and *yogis* hold in their hearts One

Who drained all poison from her, that one

like a demoness; lifting His foot so lying

Sakadam was destroyed and then taking

His rest upon that serpent of the flood...

they from sleep rise and now their blood

is also rising, and hearts rejoice as Hari

is praised... all hail our Goddess Parvai!

Simple girl, haven't you heard twittering

everywhere, the blackbird's fine singing?

Haven't you heard the sound of churning

of buttermilk while maids', hair flinging
fragrance, necklaces side to side tossed.
O noble maid, why are you to sleep lost
when we are sing to Him, to Narayana
Who has come now to us... as Krishna?
O mistress of our ways in the country...
open door! All hail our Goddess Parvai!

O cousin, fast asleep on soft cushions,
in a brightly jeweled hall, lamp shines,
incense is rising... the bars be opening
of those jeweled doors! O... be rousing
her my auntie, is your daughter stupid?
Is your daughter deaf? If she sleeps I bid
you to wake her with some incantation,
wake her from sleep, use your station...
we cry to Mathavan, Lord of Vaikuntai,
all names! All hail our Goddess Parvai!

JAYADEVA (circa 1200 AD.) He was a Sanskrit poet and most known for his composition, the epic poem *Gita Govinda,* which depicts the divine love of Krishna, an avatar of Vishnu, and his consort, Radha. This poem is considered an important text in the Bhakti movement of Hinduism. Jayadeva was born to a Hindu Brahmin family in Kenduli Sasan (formerly Kendubilva), in the Prachi valley, Puri district in Odisha. Kenduli Sasan is a village near the famous temple city of Puri. At the time of Jayadeva's birth, Odisha was under the rule of the Eastern Ganga dynasty king, Chodaganga Deva. During the reign of this monarch and his son and successor, Raghava, Jayadeva composed his Sanskrit epics. Chodaganga Deva, originally a *Shaiva,* was strongly influenced by the devotion to Krishna in and around Puri and became a *Vaishnava* devotee of Krishna himself.

The poet's parents were named *Bhojadeva* and *Ramadevi.* From temple inscriptions it is now known that Jayadeva received his education in Sanskrit poetry from a place called Kurmapataka, possibly near Konark in Odisha. Later on, Jayadeva married Padmavati, who according to temple inscriptions, may have been an accomplished temple dancer in her own right.

Prachi valley has a long history of worshipping Madhava,

another name for Krishna. During Jayadeva's life, it was known as a religious place dominated by Vaishnava Brahmins. Even today, the village of Kenduli Sasan is replete with images of Madhava. Undoubtedly, the great poet must have been influenced by the devotional milieu in that area when he composed his magnum opus, the *Gita Govinda*.

Inscriptions at Lingaraj temple, and the more recently discovered Madhukeswar temple and Simhachal temple that were read and interpreted by Dr. Satyanarayan Rajaguru have shed some light on Jayadeva's early life. These inscriptions narrate how Jayadeva had been a member of the teaching faculty of the school at Kurmapataka. He might have studied there as well. It must have been right after his childhood education in Kenduli Sasan that he left for Kurmapataka and gained experience in composing poetry, music and dancing.

Jayadeva was instrumental in popularizing the *Dasavatara,* the ten incarnations of Vishnu in another composition, *Dasakritikrite.* Furthermore, the classic *Tribhangi* (threefold) posture of Krishna playing the flute gained popularity due to him. Two hymns composed by Jayadeva have been incorporated in the *Guru Granth Sahib,* the holy book of the Sikh religion. Although it is not clear how these medieval Oriya hymns found their way to the Sikh religion, there are records narrating how Jayadeva's work had a profound influence on Guru Nanak during his visit to Puri.

The *Gita Govinda* is organized into twelve chapters. Each chapter is further sub-divided into twenty four divisions called *Prabandhas* that contain couplets grouped into eights, called *Ashtapadis*. The text also elaborates the eight moods of the heroine, the *Ashta Nayika* in its verses, which over the years has been an inspiration for many paintings, compositions and choreographic works in Indian classical dances. The work delineates the love of Krishna for Radha, the milkmaid *(gopi)*, his faithlessness and subsequent return to her, and is taken as symbolical of the human soul's straying from its true allegiance but returning at length to God Who created it. The *Gita Govinda* has been translated to many languages throughout the world and is considered to be among the finest examples of Sanskrit poetry.

Further Reading...

Gita Govinda: The Dance of Divine Love of Jayadeva Translated by Puran Singh & Paul Smith, New Humanity Books, Campbells Creek, 2013.
The Gita Govinda by Jayadeva, Translated by Sir Edwin Arnold 1792, Reprint New Humanity Books, Melbourne, 1990.
Gita Govinda Kavya of Jayadeva with The Text in Sanskrit and A Rendering in English by S. Lakshminarasimha Sastri, V. Ramaswamy Sastrulu & Sons, Madras, 1956.
The Song of Divine Love (Gita-Govinda) of Sri Jayadeva Translated by Duncan Greenlees, Kalakshetra Publications, Madras, 1957.
Gita Govinda by Jayadeva Translated from the Sanskrit by Colin John Holcombe, Ocaso Press Ltd. Santiago, 2008.
Wikipedia Article.
Love Song of the Dark Lord (Gita Govinda) of Jayadeva Translated by Barbara Stoler Miller, Colorado University Press, 1978.
Song of Love: Gita Govinda, The Sanskrit Classic Translated & Illustrated by George Keyt, Hind Pocket Books, 1960.
Kangra Paintings of the Gita Govinda by M.S. Randhawa, National Museum, New Delhi, 1963.
The Gita Govinda of Jayadeva, Translated by Monika Varma, Writers Workshop Calcutta, 1968.
Unveiling the Garden of Love: Mystical Symbolism in Layla Majnun & Gita Govinda by Lalita Sinha, World Wisdom Books, 2008

Gita Govinda

Introduction

"Sky is cloudy above dense *tamala* trees' dark loam,
it is night, O Radha, so take home young Krishna,"
Nanda spoke... so, Radha and Madhava* did roam
their divine way along Yamuna's banks, in rapture.

With his genius adorned by the hand of Saraswati,*
as a prince of poets due to devotion to Padmavati,*
this poet Jayadeva begins this story to be singing...
the description of Vasudeva's* passionate playing.

All of you, reading or hearings these songs of Hari,*
tender, sweet and passionate, full of meaning too...
take them deep inside so that to be with bliss filled,
for these words of Jayadeva are with love suffused!

Umapatidhara is prolific, Sarana isn't understood,
Goverdhana has no equal if romantically singing...
after hearing it once, Dhoyi can recite it perfectly;
but, only Jayadeva is mastery to poetry bringing.*

Notes: Madhava... Krishna. Saraswati... the goddess of learning and the arts. Padmavati... the wife of Jayadeva. Vasudeva... Krishna. Umapatidhara, Sarana, Goverdhana, Dhoyi... all brother poets of Jayadeva at the court of Laksmanasena of Bengal (circa, 1168).

Third Song of Radha's maid

I know where Krishna stays in these early days of spring,

wind from warm Malaysia brings fragrance on its wing;

brings fragrance stolen far away from thickets of clove,

in jungles where bees hum and cuckoo flutes her love,

He dances with all those *gopis* fluting a joyful tune...

all in the budding springtime, for it is sad to be alone.

I know how Krishna passes the hours of blue and gold,

when parted lovers sigh to meet, greet... closely hold

and hand in hand and each branch on the *vakul*-tree

droops with a hundred blooms, in every bloom a bee;

dancing with the *gopis* to a laughter-moving tone...

in soft awakening springtime, it's hard to live alone.

Where *kroona*-flowers open by lover's lightest tread,
from what they hear, white blushes to a modest red;
and all spears on all boughs of all the *ketuk*-glades
ready to pierce hearts of wandering youths, maids;
there Krishna dances until the merry drum is done,
in the sunny springtime, when who can live alone?

Where breaks blossom on the golden *keshra*-sprays
dazzles like Kama's staff, whom the world obeys;
patal-buds fill drowsy bees from sweet pink bowls,
as Kama's goblet steeps in languor human souls...
He dances with them, of Badha no thinking's done,
in warm new springtide when none will live alone.

Where Madhvi breathes incenses through the grove,
and silken Mogras lull sense with essences of love,
silk-soft pale Mogra, whose perfume fine and faint
can melt coldness of a maid, sternness of a saint...
dances with the *gopis,* your other self... your One,
in the sleepy springtime when none will live alone.

As if warm lips touched eyes to wake them, the bloom

opens upon the mangoes... to feel the sunshine come;

and... *atimuktas* wind arms of softest green about

clasping stems, calm, clear great Jamuna spreads out;

there dances, laughs your Love, with many a one...

in rosy days of springtime, He will not live alone.

Fourth Song... by Radha (free-form translation)

In this forest I meditate on Him,

my Beloved!

How His lips incarnadined

pour out floods of melody.

I see His flute at His lips

and His fingers on His flute:

ah...

His moving fingers touch my heart!

How His earrings shake

with the liquid rhythm

of His trembling flute!

His laughing eyes,

His waving forehead,

His dancing flesh!

I think of Him
Whose presence puts these brides
into a maddening frenzy of Love!
I think of Him
Who is dancing perfection
with a hundred brides!
He is my Krishna!

O my friend,
take me to Him,
that like a lover's meeting
is concealed in secret places,
and Who is now satiated
with the joy of dancing!

Take me to Him
from these groves of trees
whose leaves shade me
and separate me from Him.

I am mad with love,

my mind wanders in all directions for Him,

my flesh quivers with the pain of that

rare passion for Him...

O let me meet my Krishna,

now!

O friend,

take me to Him

Whose beauty unlaces all my garments,

remembering Him makes my song

sweet and lovely...

Who through one glance

takes me into Himself

and Himself into me,

Who weds me without ceremony...

a new wedding with every meeting

with Him.

I think of Krishna

Who still stands apart from all

under the *kadamba* tree!

O my friend,

tell me what I should do!

My mind renounces me and goes to Him

Who is fond of dancing with a hundred brides.

O what can I do?

My mind can find no fault in Him

for it is always busy thinking of His beauty.

O what can I do?

Even if in my pride

I turn away from Him

I still can do nothing but think of Him.

O my friend,

I can no more live here!

Take me to Him

Whose beauty makes me surrender my all,

for ever...

O let me now meet my Krishna!

O my friend,

take me to Him

Who gathered me in His arms

and kissed me

as I sat in my bed of forest leaves

and Who lay for hours in rapture

resting on my bosom...

and Who has tasted the devotion

of my lips.

O let me now meet my Krishna!

O my friend,

take me to Him

Whose temples translucent with

the glow of passion

and Whose eyes are closing

with the ecstasy of joys...

and Whose body is moist

after the dance.

O let me now meet my Krishna!

O my friend,

my head is strewn with flowers

and my voice is grown sweet as a cuckoo's

and this breast of mine has felt

the touch of His fingertips

soothing my flesh

and my being already knows

(in my imagination) the joy of union!

O let me now meet my Krishna!

O my friend,

jewelled anklets ring on my feet

and around my small waist hangs

the singing girdle of silver bells…

let me lie in His embrace

Who knows the joy of me,

and Who maddened by my sweetness

holds me by the hair,

raises my face to Himself

and imprints a kiss on me

already in my intense thought of Him.

O, I tremble and shake with love!

JANABAI (1263-1350) Janabai was born in Gangakhed, Maharashtra to a couple with first names Rand and Karand. Under the caste system which rigidly existed in India, the couple belonged to the lowest caste. After her mother died her father took her to Pandharpur. From her childhood Janabai worked as a maidservant in the household of Damasheti, who lived in Pandharpur and who was the father of the prominent Marathi religious poet Namdev (see his section following). Janabai cared for the young Namdev and remained his *Daasi* (a servant) throughout her life. She would call herself *Naamyasi Daasi* (servant of Namdev) It is said that they died on the same day.

Pandharpur has high religious significance especially among Marathi-speaking Hindus. Janabai's employers, Damasheti and his wife, Gonai, were very religious. Through the influence of the religious environment around her and her innate inclination, Janabai was all along an ardent devotee of Lord Vitthal (Krishna as a child) and she was also gifted with poetic talent. Though she never had any formal schooling, she thus composed many high-quality religious verses of the *abhang* form. Fortunately, some of her compositions got preserved along with those of Namdev. Authorship of about 340 *abhangs* is traditionally attributed to Janabai.

Janabai's poetry is replete with her love for God. It is said that because of her devotion to God, she completely succeeded in merging into God by erasing herself. She became detached even before she realized God. She has sketched innumerable of her experiences in life in her compositions. Her compositions are replete with her devotional love for he Guru Saint Namdev, her intense love towards Saint Dnyaneshwar, the great devotional strength of Saint Chokhamela and her devotion towards Lord Vitthal. She has indeed done her future generations a great favour by doing a precise of the life, good characteristics and great work of the great saints in her time like Saint Dnyaneshwar, Saint Namdev, Saint Sopankaka, Saint Goroba, Saint Chokha Mela, Saint Sen Nhavi, etc.

Her simple language touches the heart of the common man. Along with Dnyaneshwar, Namdev, Eknath and Tukaram, Janabai has a revered place in the minds of Marathi-speaking Hindus.

Further Reading...

Mysticism in Maharashtra by R.D. Ranade, Motilal Banarsidass, Delhi, 1933.

Images of Women in Maharashtrian Literature and Religion, Anne Feldhaus (Editor), State University of New York State Press, Albany 1996.

Women Saints in World Religions, Arvind Sharma (Editor) McGill Studies in the Histories of Religions, State University of New York State Press, Albany 2000. (Pages 145-180).

Women Writing in India: 600 B.C. to the Present, V: 600 B.C. to the Early Twentieth Century, Edited by Susie Tharu & K. Lalita, The Feminist Press, City University of New York, 1991.

(Pages 82-3).

Stories of Indian Saints (A Translation of Mahipati's Marathi poem Bhakta-Vijaya) by Justin E. Abbot & Pandit Narhar R. Godbole Vols 1 & 11, Motilal Banarsidass, Delhi, 1933. (Pages 338 et al).

Saints of Maharashtra by Savitribai Khanolkar, Bharatiya Vidya Bhavan, Bombay, 1978. (Pages 50-4).

Abhangs…

Here, let me be born as often as You are wanting:
but, let it be that all my desires You are fulfilling!
I desire to see Pandharpur, am Namdev serving,
even if a cat or a bird, or dog, or pig I'm becoming.
My condition is that in each life that I am living
I have to see Pandarpur and Namdev be serving!
It is the ambition of Namdev's maid I'm saying!

O Hari, give to me, this poor girl, this only:
Your holy Name alone, will be sung by me!
My desire fulfill that You will accepting be
of my humble prayers and service, my plea!
Eyes and mind on You I always want to see
and on my lips have Your name for eternity:
at Your feet for this is falling the maid Jani!

Vitthali, that thief of Pandhari I caught
by tying a rope around His neck... tight.
Then, I locked Him up tight in my heart,
and with the Word I tied tight His feet!
With the words, "I am Him," I repeat...
I thrashed, I beat Him... Who I caught!
Vitthal complained bitterly and sought
freedom: Jani, "Chances, are nought!"

Divine is what I eat and what I'm drinking:
bed of mine is divine, divine's in everything.
There's nothing with divine not overflowing!
Jani: "Vitthal, all from inside out is filling!"

Jani is sick of *karma*, but... debt how to repay?
You leave Your divinity to me pound all day!
You came to wash my clothes and me away...
as woman, with hands You get dung and hay.
O Lord, at Your feet I want a place to stay...
this says Jani, the servant of Namdev, today

If Ganges to ocean flows, and away ocean turns her,
Vitthal, now tell me who would her complaints hear?
Can fish river be rejecting, can mother child not bear?
Jani says, "You must accept who to You surrender!"

O Lord of Pandhari, what now should I be doing?
Time is not with me, in a strange land I'm living!
Kesava... I can only to You my cries be bringing:
You're my refuge, me only You can be consoling.
I'm a helpless girl! Jani says: "Me be protecting!"

To end of the horizon the bird flies,
and for its chicks food inside it lies.
Across the sky a mother-eagle flies,
but... back to her young she retires,
To finish her work the mother tries,
but mind from baby never away lies.
The mother monkey over a tree flies,
her baby holding her stomach, tries.
The same way mother Vitthal spies
Jani, again and again and... no lies!

This one, is in that highest joy grounded...

consciousness of form has totally vanished.

Once one this divine sleep has experienced

one never wakes again to acts of the world.

When one's complete being is so blessed...

in void even memory of subtle-form is dead.

Jani is gone, that oneness having attained!

Jani, tired, hungry went to do washing by the river:

behind her, Vitthal ran and He began to beg her...

"Why don't you be taking Me with you, I implore!"

Jani asked, "God, why run like this, never before?"

Vitthal, the real essence of the world, looked at her

all bashful, kept following her, not a word, I swear!

Once, in the middle of the night, Vitthal arrived...

Namdev said, "Look Who at the door's arrived!"

With the divine light the whole house overflowed:

all were waking, Vitthal and Jani then embraced.

Namdev, then proclaimed... "Jani is so blessed!"

God, I no longer have any fascination for You:

I'm not going to be anymore serving only You!
You are no longer compassionate... it is true!
The false pride of greatness is carried by You!
Being angry with me, gains You nothing, true!
We're why You're strong, I thought You knew!
Of Your own You've no power! We help You!
God... do I not understand Your secret? I do!

I gained everything that I had wanted...
the serpent of Vishnu, me, had blessed!
I was to an awareness beyond body led:
blessed with eternal peace, 'I' vanished!
The source of anger in me He crushed...
in me all knowledge... He established!
Refuge in Him Vitthal to me granted...
Jani says, "God is gracious... indeed!"

Everywhere, Krishna I am seeing:
I look left... Krishna, I am seeing!
Krishna, when right I am looking:
down and at Krishna I'm looking!
All I see, not moving or moving...
only Krishna is to be recognizing!

I'm where? Me, I'm not recalling!

NAMDEV (1270-1350). Namdev (or Namdeo, or Namdeva) was born in the village of Narasi-Bamani, now located in the Hingoli District in Maharashta, to a tailor named Damasheti Relekar and his wife Gonai. Yadusheth, his ancestor in the seventh generation, was a devotee of *Bhagawad-Dharma*. Soon after his birth, his family moved to Pandharpur, where the prominent temple of Lord Vithoba (Krishna as a boy) is located. Saint Namdev's spent the better part of his life of eighty years at Pandharpur. His parents were devotees of Vithoba.

Namdev who was a contemporary of Saint Dnyaneshwar (see his section following) is considered a prominent religious poet of Maharashtra. He was one the earliest writers who wrote in the Marathi language. He is the foremost proponent of the *Bhagwad-Dharma* who reached beyond Maharashtra into the Punjab. He also wrote some hymns in Hindi and Punjabi. Namdev established religious unity across the country.

According to a legend, when Namdev was five years old his mother once gave him some food offerings for Vithoba and asked him to give it to Vithoba in the Pandharpur temple. Namdev took the offerings and placed it before Vithoba's idol in the temple, asking Vithoba to accept the offerings. When he saw that his request was not being met, he told Vithoba that he would kill himself if Vithoba continued to ignore the offerings. Vithoba then appeared before him and ate the offerings in response to the utter devotion of young Namdev.

At the age of eleven Namdev was married to Rajai. Namdev and Rajai had four sons namely Nara, Vitha, Gonda, Mahada and a daughter called Limbai. His elder sister Aubai also lived with them. There were in all fifteen people in the household. The year 1291 was a turning point in his life at the age of twenty-one when he met Saint Dnyaneshwar. He accepted Visoba Khechar as his ultimate *Guru*, through whom he actually saw the form of God.

Namdev travelled through many parts of India, reciting his religious poems. In difficult times he played the difficult role of uniting the people of Maharashtra spiritually. He is said to have lived for more than twenty years in the village of Ghuman in the Gurdaspur district of Punjab. He composed around 125 *abhangs* in Hindi. Sixty-one of these came to be included in Sikh Scripture, the *Guru Granth Sahib*. In his early fifties, Namdev settled down at Pandharpur where he gathered around himself a group of devotees. His *abhangs* became very popular and people thronged to listen to his

Kirtan. Approximately 2500 of Namdev's *abhangs* have been collected in *Namdev Vaachi Gatha*. The book also includes the long autobiographical poem *Teerthaavali*, talking about his travels in the company of Saint Dnyaneshwar (see his section to follow next). This poem makes him the first autobiographer in Marathi literature. Saint Namdev is regarded to have had a significant influence on Saint Tukaram (to follow later).

Further Reading…

The Hindi Padavali of Namdev, A Critical Edition of Namdev's Hindi Songs with Translation & Annotation by Winand M. Callewaert & Mukund Lath, Motilal Banarsidass Publishers Pvt. Ltd., New Delhi, India, 1989
Namdev: His Mind and Art by R. N. Maurya, Bahri Publications, New Delhi, 1988.
Saint Namdev by J.R. Puri & V.K. Sethi, Radha Soami Satsang Beas, Punjab, 1978.
Saint Namdev by Prof. M.A. Karandikar, Maharashtra Information Centre, Bombay, 1985.
Sufis, Mystics and Yogis of India by Bankey Behari, Bharatiya Vidya Bhavan, Bombay, 1962. (Pages 252-260).
Religion and Public Memory: A Cultural History of Saint Namdev by Christian Lee Novetzke, Columbia University Press, 2011.

Abhangs...

Strange! Sometimes He gives sweets to His devotee;
the next day one might get nothing, not even one pea!
The following day he may get grain on floor, all dusty:
such is God's love for His devotee... and His Glory!
One day He confers on one a horse to ride, fine to see:
the next one has to walk barefoot on the path, happily.
One day a beautiful bed is there for one who is sleepy,
the next even the earth's denied, yet joyful is devotee!
All is the blessing of the Master, if Him one does see:
Namdeva states... one crosses cycle of rebirth, surely.

Once Namdev, heart devoted, Lord's temple visited:
from enthusiasm he forgot all... ecstatically danced!
A priest, irritated by his dance, him outside pushed:
"My birth as a low-caste, You gave," I complained.
The Lord, pleased with him, his prayer answered...
the front of the temple He to the back then turned!
Namdev pleased by this a song to the Lord started:
all witnessing this miracle to Namdev then bowed!

Namdev's hut in a great fire was burnt up one day,
our Lord Hari came and repaired it straight away!
The new thatched roof brought neighbours its way:
if Namdev could build one for them… they'd pay!
"Builder of my roof, was Hari," Namdev did say.
"Only love and total surrender for it, is His pay…
renouncing family, possessions… any other way!
Then, He rushes to that one, so joyful is that day!
Omnipotent, omniscient, He is Lord in every way!
To explain all He does is impossible for one to say.
He is body, life, soul of Namdeva who does pray;
surrendering at His lotus feet, completely today."

My mind is like the measuring stick of the tailor…
and this tongue of mine could be likened to a scissor.
The cloth of life with this mind of mine I measure…
with tongue I cut it, of His Name I am a repeater!
About my caste, saying His Name, I'm no worrier:
I dye that cloth, with His Name of it I'm a sewer!
All I know is that the Lord's Name's my supporter:
Worshiping the Lord… of His praises I'm a singer!
I contemplate my Lord Protector, Him I remember!

The needle's made of gold and the string is of silver!

Namdev with His Name, day and night is a sewer.

Omnipotent and omniscient, He is wherever I'm looking:

His power in this illusion is difficult to be understanding.

Everything is Govinda, from Govinda comes everything:

without Govinda* there is nothing that is truly existing!

Not any different from the ocean is froth, bubbles flying:

the creation is His Game that He enters and is playing!

This world and all things in it are illusory... be knowing.

When the Master the torch of wisdom to me was giving,

the Truth behind all of creation to me He was revealing.

I now live in the Lord's Creation... always remembering

Lord Murari* Who always in all is, Namdev is saying.

*Note: Govinda... Lord Vishnu, sometimes Krishna. Lord Murari... Lord
Vishnu, Krishna.

All are busy being cunning, but none the game play

with a detachment that the inner fever takes away!

Mankind looks after only the physical, every day...

but inside their hearts are like devils, burning away.

The All-knowing One no one knows, it's sad to say:

without One it's a dream, awake, asleep, night, day!
He who is learning to the flame hold, like a bouquet,
such a one is a saint, a sage... a knower of the Way!
Only that devote done who sings His Name all day
in his heart attains liberation... Namdev does say!

Only one word in the world is everlasting...
that word 'Hari' is my life, my everything.
A real devotee is not affected by anything
that colours a world that is really nothing.
The devotee, is one who cares not a thing
for path the world travels upon! Nothing!
Rare is one who true liberation is knowing:
in lies, delusion all are lost... not-knowing!
To the absolute Truth Namdev is bowing:
Perfect Master is near you they are saying.

The name of Lord Rama* this heart has entered...
and now the golden scale inside it has been placed.
In the sky one flies a paper kite one has constructed:
though to friends talking on string mind's fastened.
A full pot of water a real princess balances on head:
laughing, she claps hands... mind to pot is still led.

A shed has ten doors, cows leave to feed or be fed...
cow grazes for miles, mind on calf back in the shed.
Child's in cradle, mother in her room working hard:
on child's her mind, Namdev says: have you heard?

Note: Lord Rama, the Avatar of Vishnu, as is Lord Krishna.

Why be dancing and singing... again and again?
Why put on sandalwood paste, again and again?
Real Self from the other you can't tell, it's plain:
by what it sees mind is tricked; hard to explain!
Before idol people dance for some kind of gain...
never knowing their true Self, lies in their frame.
If only you knew how to serve the One, the same
One as you, your vision would see the All, again!
Namdev says: I only am worshipping that same
One in me and nothing else: am I talking plain?

Why be meditating and prayers be muttering
when the real One in you, you go on ignoring?
Serpent drops its skin, but poison is keeping:
only in looks a *yogi*, heron stands meditating.
From a lion, can the slow prey ever be hiding?
All this is about the false gods worshipping!

The Lord of Namdev all conflict is silencing.
You hypocrite, medicine of Rama be drinking.

If I should be telling the truth they will kill me:
against the many, one always the loser will be.
A word of the truth can disperse an assembly:
it can break bones and ridicule and hurt many!
Many people the dirt in their minds don't see:
they place faith in soap and water... stupidly!
In bright clothes and keeping bad company...
these hypocrites shame themselves... nightly.
All these fools put on a show, until suddenly
death's noose is tight on neck until dead is he.
Namadev says... these are sinful fools, see...
they don't remember the Lord, unfortunately.

Govind is my mother, Govind is my father:
Govind is my castle, caste and my Master.
Govind is my knowledge, and my prayer...
my constant source of bliss, is Lord Rama!
Govind is a singer and Govind is a dancer:
dressed as Govind I'm dancing on, forever.

I offer all to Him, of Him I'm a worshipper:

Namdev says… of a God, I have no other!

DNYANESHWAR (1275-1296). Dnyaneshwar, (sometimes called Jnadeva), was born in Maharashtra before the Muslim invasions of the region started. During this period, arts and sciences prospered under the patronage of the newly ascended Yadava kings. However, this period also witnessed religious degeneration, superstitions and rituals which involved animal sacrifices and worship of many deities. Dnyaneshwar emerged as one the first original philosophers and poets to write in the Marathi language.

He was the second of the four children of Vitthal Govind Kulkarni and Rukmini, a pious couple from Apegaon near Paithan on the banks of the river Godavari. Vitthal had studied Vedas and set out on pilgrimages at a young age.

In Alandi, about 30 km from Pune, Sidhopant, a local Yajurveda Brahmin, was very much impressed with him and Vitthal married his daughter Rukmini. Four children were born to them; Nivrutti in 1273, Dnyaneshwar in 1275, Sopan in 1277 and daughter Mukta in 1279. The children became orphaned and grew up as beggars. They approached the Brahmin community of Paithan to accept them but the Brahmins refused. Their argument with the Brahmins earned the children fame and respect due to their righteousness, virtue, intelligence, knowledge and politeness.

Dnyaneshwar became the student of Nivrutti (his older brother) along with his younger siblings Sopan and Mukta at the age of 8. He learnt and mastered the philosophy and various techniques of yoga. Dnyaneshwar began his literary work when Nivrutti instructed him to write a commentary on *Bhagavad Gita*, the *Dnyaneshwari* or *Bhavartha Deepika*. The wonderful commentary was completed when Dnyaneshwar was only 15 years old! Considered a masterpiece of Marathi literature, the 18 chapters are composed in 'ovi'... *slokas*.

Dnyaneshwar liberated the 'divine knowledge' locked in the Sanskrit language to bring that knowledge into *Prakrit* (Marathi) and made it available to the common man.

Amrutanubhavu written some time after, contains 10 chapters and 806 *ovi*. The basis of this book is non-dualism (*advaita siddhanta*).

After the early *Samadhi* of Dnyaneshwar, Nivrutti travelled with his sister Mukta on a pilgrimage along the Tapi river where they were caught in a thunderstorm and Mukta was swept away. Nivrutti took to salvation (*Samadhi*) at Tryambakeshwar. Around 375 *abhangs* a form of devotional poetry sung in praise of Vithoba (the child Krishna) are attributed to him.

Sopandev was a younger brother. Sopandev attained 'samadhi' at Saswad near Pune. He wrote a book 'Sopandevi' based on the *Bhagvadgita's* Marathi interpretation along with 50 or so *abhangas.*

Muktabai, the youngest, was known for her simple and straightforward expression of thoughts. She could be considered as one of the first poetesses in Marathi along with Mahadamba. There are around 40 *abhangs* attributed to her.

After having composed *Amrutanubhau*, Dnyaneshwar made a pilgrimage to northern India with Namdev (see previously) and other saints. After completing this pilgrimage he expressed his intention to enter into a state of *Samadhi* because he felt that the mission of his life was complete.

At the age of 21 Dnyaneshwar entered into a permanent state of *Sanjeevan Samadhi* at Alandi in Maharashtra.

Further Reading...

The Philosophy of Jnanadeva, As Gleaned from the Amrutanubhava by B.P. Bahirat, Motilal Banarsidass, Delhi, 1956.

The Jnaneshwari (Bhavarth Dipika) Translated from the Marathi by M.R. Yardi, Bharatiya Vidya Bhavan, Pune, 1991.

Jnaneshvari (Bhavarthadipika), A Song-sermon on the Bhagavadgita translated from the Marathi by V.G. Pradhan, Edited by H.M. Lambert, 2 vols. George Allen & Unwin, London, 1966.

Amrutanubhau, The Nectar of Divine Experience by Sri Dnyaneshwar, Translated by Madhava, Ajay Prakashan, Pune, 1981.

Slokas from the 'Amrutanubhau' Chapter Nine.

And now, all fragrance has become the nose…
ears have become words, mirrors are the eyes.
And, the blowing breeze a fan was becoming,
head was the champak flower, scent blowing!
And, the sweetest flavour the tongue became
chakor-bird was moon, lotus the sun became.
Then, the form of the bee became the flower,
girl became boy and bed became the sleeper.
Mango leaf became the cuckoo, and the body
hills of Malaya's fragrance, tongue… syrupy!
It was like a piece of pure gold made of itself
was engraving ornaments, so enjoying itself.
So… the enjoyer and the object of enjoyment,
seer and object of sight are one in the present.
Into a thousand petals blooms *sevanti* flower
without it not still being… the *sevanti* flower!
Although beating are drums of new experience
in town of inactivity ears… them, don't sense.

So the multitude of the senses simultaneously
will run to the objects before them, instantly.
But when one looks in mirror, mirror vanishes;
it is the same with desires, sense disappears!
Although three, ornament, bangle and earring:
one who buys, really only gold is purchasing.
And, if a hand to gather ripples should reach,
it'll be discovered there is only water in each!
As camphor presents itself as only fragrance,
so only God is vibrating in every appearance.
So, when the hands in form of various senses
like ears are ready like words to get pleasures,
when object and senses make contact, object
is no more of senses, God is the only contact!
So all sticks of the sugarcane have sweetness,
full moon has all from the new moon one sees.
The senses and the objects coming together…
is like moonlight on moon or upon sea, water.

Even though that one is continuing speaking,
his spiritual meditation he is not disturbing.
His inner actionless condition isn't affected,
although countless actions he has performed.

As organs of senses the ordinary are enjoying
no pleasure is greater than the inner enjoying.
Uncountable arms of sun are spread to collect
the dark, but they sun being sun do not affect.
As, in a dream one desires to meet a woman,
but when one wakes one is alone... one man!
So when one of spiritual wisdom does witness
sensual objects, we don't know if them he sees.
If the moon wanted to gather the moonlight
what's it done? Imagination without result!
Yoga of yogis of sense-restraint is worthless
besides path of wisdom... as moon in day is!
There is no action or inaction and everything
and all as God's experience keeps happening.
One of unity, of own accord duality enters...
the unity's deeper, as greater the differences!
Enjoyment of objects is sweeter than unity...
in home of union devotee is devoted, utterly.
Even if that one's walking in the street or he
is sitting just still, always in his house is he.
There is no goal though he may do anything,
if he does nothing... his goal he is achieving.
No room for forgetfulness or memory is here:

in this condition such behaviour is quite rare.
Whatever he wants is natural, a meditation...
quality of this stage is the glory of salvation.
The Almighty then the devotee is becoming,
goal is the way; universe, one alone sitting.
He may be God or devotee, at any moment:
he enjoys kingdom of inaction each moment.
The temple merges in God... pervading all:
the flow of time and space is vanishing: all!

In Himself, God contains His own being...
no place for goddess, attendants in waiting.
Now one may desire the pupil and master,
only God can be employed to be each other.
Devotion, repeating His name, meditation,
all belief disappear: existing is God, alone!
God's worshipping God with the Almighty
in form of any offering, all is the Almighty!
Temple, idol, attendants, all from same rock
are carved; so, acts of devotion do not mock.
A tree has no other existence than to spread
in the form of its foliage, fruit, flowers, shade.
If a dumb person observes silence or not, it is

not wonderful; so, the wise, praying or not is!
Goddess made of rice is worshipped, not rice:
so should she be worshipped by grains of rice?
And will the flame of a lamp remain uncovered
if we are not asking it... to become uncovered?
Is not the moon totally covered with her light,
though we don't ask her to wear her moonlight?
It's natural for the fire to be throwing out heat,
so why should we think of making it give heat?
God is the wise one worshipping God alone...
while worshipping or not He remains the One.
Lights of action and inaction are now finished,
devotion and non-devotion one meal, finished.
Sacred texts of the Upanishads are censured,
but censure itself becomes a hymn, treasured.
Both praise and censure are to silence reduced:
if words are said... they are silently produced.
A pilgrimage to God though He's everywhere:
if one is going to God the journey is nowhere!
In a state like this it's wonderful that walking
and sitting in one place... the same are being.
If that one sees an object any time in any way
that one has the joy of seeing God in that way.

Though God is seen before that one, it is like
that one saw nothing as God and he are alike.
Of its own volition a ball falls and hits itself
and rebounds and is in bliss of... its own Self!
If it was possible to see a ball at play like that
we could talk of the wise one's play, like that!
Knowledge can't know, action can't touch it...
spontaneous devotion continues, as it sees fit!
It's endless and in itself it is goes on and on...
Compared to this, any other bliss can go on?
The wonderful secret of true devotion, this is:
where meditation and knowledge unite this is.
Shiva and Vishnu, really are identical... here;
difference in their names and forms unite here.
Shiva, Shakti that each other were swallowing,
here them at the same time One is swallowing.
Here, the Word... all objects is eating, and all
kinds of speech is drinking, resting in the All!
O blessed, powerful Lord, You have made us
the sovereign of the kingdom of Divine bliss!
It is wonderful You awakened those waking,

laid to sleep all sleeping, us... made realizing.

All in all we are Yours, out of love You call

us Yours... Your greatness is in such a call.

You do not take anything, to none give You.

Your greatness we don't know how to get to.

As a Master You are the supreme Light, for

you help devotee... drowning in life's water!

If Your unity was affected while It sharing,

Your greatness Vedas wouldn't be praising!

Highest One, You have become my relative

by removing any difference, unity You give!

LALLA DED (1320-1392). Lalla Ded, Lalleshwari or Lallayogeshwari, is the famous female poet/saint from Kashmir who lived at *exactly* the same time as the incomparable Hafiz of Shiraz. Her *vakhs* (poem-sayings) are sung even today in Kashmir. Born in Pandrethan, near Srinagar, she was married at a young age, but the marriage was a failure and she walked out at the age of twenty four. She became a disciple of Siddha Srikantha (Sed Bayu). It must have taken a lot of courage on her part to walk out of a marriage and to walk around unclothed as she did. She was treated with contempt by some and with extreme respect and reverence by others, seeing her as a saint and eventually as a Spiritual Master.

Her *vakhs* or sayings numbering around two hundred are some of the oldest examples of Kashmiri in written form that have come down to us. She was a bridge between Hindu mysticism and Sufism. Muslims knew her as Lalla Arifa and Hindus as Lalleshwari. Lalla Ded is supposed to have suckled when a baby Sheikh Noorudin the Sufi mystic who was known as Nand Rishi to the Hindus of Kashmir. Her poems are more influential today than they have ever been, not only in Kashmir but around the world.

Further Reading...

Lalla Ded: Selected Poems, Translation & Introduction Paul Smith, New Humanity Books Campbells Creek, 2012.
Mystical Verses of Lalla: A Journey of Self Realization, Translated by Jaishree Kak, Illustrations by Joseph Singer. Motilal Banarsidass Publishers, New Delhi, 2007.
Lal Ded by Jayalal Kaul, S. Akademi, New Delhi, 1973.
Lalla-Vakyani: or The Wise Sayings of Lal Ded. Edited and translated by Sir George Grierson and Lionell D. Barnett, Royal Asiatic Society, London, 1920.
To the Other Shore: Lalla's Life and Poetry, Jaishere Kaik Odin, Vitasta, New Delhi, 1999.
The Religion and Teachings of Lalla, by Richard Carnac Temple, Vintage Books, New Delhi, 1990.

Vakhs...

One has to endure cloudbursts and lightning,

or at noon the sudden darkness that comes...

or the body that two grindstones are crushing.

With patience, accept it, contentment comes!

In the mortar of love, my heart I ground;

I calmed down after evil thoughts left...

I tasted it, after it, I roasted and burned!

By doing this, will I die... or alive be left?

At dawn I woke, with my restless mind I called;

I withstood pain then to God I turned, saying:

"I'm Lalla, Lalla, Lalla," and woke my Beloved.

With that One, mind and body I kept purifying.

I was abused and slandered, I put up with it all:

of my past and present... scandals everywhere!

I'm Lalla: this longing of mine rose, not to fall.
My goal I attained, of nothing else was aware.

On many paths, soles of my feet I wore away:
only one path was revealing the truth to me.
Why aren't all hearing this fascinated, today?
Lalla only one word in a hundred heard clearly.

My Master, again and again I kept on asking...
"What name has that, which can't be defined?"
Such question again and again was exhausting.
Out of this nothing... something has happened!

When to this self I was firmly attached,
from me, hidden You were still staying.
While I was seeking You, time passed:
looking in, You and I blissfully, uniting!

You are the earth... You are the sky too;
You are the night, the wind and the day:
Sandalwood, rose, water, grain, are You.
You are... all! What to offer? Please say!

You, Divine One, all of creation permeate:
You, Divine One, all of matter… enliven.
You, Divine One, without sound resonate!
Who, O One Divine, can know You, even?

Only one piece of advice my Master gave to me:
turn the consciousness inward… from the outer.
The initiation of Lalla became only this, for me:
that is the reason why I, naked, began to wander.

When… will you be remembering,
vow that in the womb, you made?
Die even before your body is dying,
at death you'll be at a higher grade.

I did not wait for the right time or trust in anything;
the wine that I, Lalla, was drinking, was my poetry.
I was catching the darkness inside and it gathering
and then I was ripping it into bits: now, do you see?

They can call me names, they can criticise me:
let them be calling me whatever they want to!
They can be offering to me flowers, devotedly:
I am not impressed, so who gains... me... you?

With thirst and starvation don't hurt your body:
be taking care of your body when it is exhausted!

On your religious rites and fasts may a curse be:
the real religion's to be good to others... instead!

I came into this world, straight...
but my return was a crooked line.
Being poor by river was my fate!
To cross over, could I pay a fine?

With a loose-spun rope my boat I am towing:
I pray God hears me, brings me across safely.
Like water in unbaked clay away I'm wasting:

O God, my one desire is to get home, help me!

Mind, I weep for you, loving the illusion:
when you are dead not even a shadow on
will go of this world when you pass on...
so why have you your real Self forgotten?

A vast pit's under you, above you dance!
Sir, tell me, how you can keep doing this?
You will leave all riches... extravagance!
O sir, your meal, how can you enjoy this?

I am a wooden bow, a rush-grass arrow,
an ignorant carpenter, a palace building:
a shop unlocked in a busy bazaar... I go
on unclean... my state who is knowing?

I came from what direction, what road:
how to know road to where I'm going?
Right guidance soon lessens my load:
an empty breath's worth... is nothing!

Bag of candy's knot is loose upon my shoulder,
my burden is so heavy... how can I now go on?
Master's words to be detached make me suffer:
a flock with no shepherd, how can I now go on?

I saw a wise man, who was of hunger dying,
as the leaves fell with winds of near winter.
Then I saw a fool who was his cook beating,
now... Lalla waits for of world ties to sever.

When the washer-man on stone slab dashed me,
with soap and washing soda rubbing harshly...
and tailor with scissors cut me up, completely,
then, I, Lalla, the ultimate bliss did experience!

From me I came out seeking the moonlight,
I went on seeking what is like with the like.
O Naryana, all is You, all is Your Light...
as all is You, how can there be any 'like'?*

Soul is always new, the moon is ever new:
I saw the universal waters… always new!
As I, Lalla, cleaned body and mind anew,
I Lalla, am ever new, ever new, new I am!

What's happened, what's become of me?
Everything I was attached to, has gone…
all of my songs are saying, continually…
I Lalla am on a lake, where's bank, home?

I sought for my Self, but, it was worthless,
the hidden knowledge not found, remained.
Then in Self I was lost, nectar was endless:
the cups were full but them no one drained!

Put on clothes that from cold protects you,
eat enough food that you won't be hungry.
Let mind concentrate upon the Self in you:
the body as food for crows of the forest see.

Into a universe of birth and rebirth I was coming,
through asceticism's light... knowledge I gained.
Death of anyone is nothing to me as is my dying:
if I live then it's fine, and fine it is if I have died!

Although some are sleep they're really all seeing;
although some are awake, they're seeing nothing.
Some after a sacred bath still unclean are staying,
and others even householders detached are being.

My Master, just one piece of advice gave me,
stop looking outside, start to look... inwardly.
That was the one rule given to Lalla, clearly:
that is the reason naked I went for all to see!

Who is fast asleep and who is wide awake?
Out from what lake... is the water oozing?
What to God can one offer... for His sake?
What is the highest state, one is attaining?

I ground up my heart in love's mortar...
I calmed down as evil thoughts left me.
I burned it away, for I had gone too far,
now what I've done to me is a mystery!

I followed what I read, but I realized
what I experienced... through living!
Lion of desires into a jackal I tamed:
I followed Truth, then was knowing.

You are the earth, You are the heavens too:
You're the night and the wind and the day!
Offering, sandalwood, flowers are all You:
You're all, so what can I offer, please say!

VIDYAPATI (1352-1448?) Vidyapati Thakur, also known by the sobriquet *Maithil Kavi Kokil* (the poet cuckoo of Maithili) was a Maithili poet and a Sanskrit writer. He was born in the village of Bishphi in Madhubani district of Bihar state, India. The name Vidyapati is derived from two Sanskrit words, *Vidya* (knowledge) and *Pati* (master), connoting thereby, *a man of knowledge.*

Vidyapati's poetry was widely influential in centuries to come, in the Hindustani as well as Bengali and other Eastern Indian literary traditions. The language at the time of Vidyapati, the *prakrit*-derived late *abahatta,* had just began transition into early versions of the Eastern languages, Bengali, Oriya, Maithili, etc. Vidyapati's influence on making these languages has been described as 'analogous to that of Dante in Italy and Chaucer in England.' Vidyapati is as much known for his love-lyrics as for his poetry dedicated to Lord Shiva. His language is closest to Maithili, the language spoken around Mithila (a region in the north Bihar), closely related to the *abahattha* form of early Bengali.

The love songs of Vidyapati, which describe the sensuous

love story of Radha and Krishna (see following), follow a long line of Vaishnav love poetry popular in Eastern India, and include much celebrated poetry such as Jayadeva's *Gita Govinda* of the 12th century (see his section previously). This tradition that uses the language of physical love to describe spiritual love, was a reflection of a key turn in Hinduism, initiated by Ramanuja in the 11th century which advocated an individual self realization through direct love. Similar to the reformation in Christianity, this movement empowered the common man to realize God directly, without the intervention of learned priests. Part of the transformation was also a shift to local languages as opposed to the formal Sanskrit of the religious texts.

The songs he wrote as prayers to Lord Shiva are still sung in Mithila and form a rich tradition of sweet and lovely folk songs. Vidyapati, mainly known for his love songs and prayers for Lord Shiva, also wrote on other topics including ethics, history, geography, and law. His other works include: *Purusa Pariksā* deals with moral teachings. *Likhanabali* is about writing. *Bhu-Parikrama*, literal meaning, around the world, is about local geography. *Vibhāgasāra* is autobiographical in nature.

Further Reading...

Love Songs of Vidyapati, Translated by Deben Bhattacharya, George Allen & Unwin Ltd, London 1963.

Vidyapati Bangiya Padabali : Songs of the Love of Radha and Krishna by Vidaypati Thakura, Translated by Ananda Coomaraswamy and Arjun Sen. The Old Bourne Press, London, 1915.

Vidayaptis Songs translated by Sri Aurobindo, 1901. Pub? 45 songs.

The poets of Bengal: Bidyapati. A comprehensive collection of his Bengali songs compiled from various ancient manuscripts and the sacred books of the Vaishnavas, with copious notes and introduction by Kaliprasanna Kavyabisharad. Secular Press, Calcutta, 1895.

Purusapariksa of Vidyapati translated by Jha Shashi Nath, Mithila Institute of Post-Graduate Studies and Research in Sanskrit Learning, 2009.

Vidyapati: The Greatest Poet of Mithila (1360-1450 A.D.) Greater Janakpur Area Development Council, Janakpurdham, 2007.

Songs of Vidyapati, Translated by Shbhadra Jha, Motilal Banarasidass, Banaras, 1954.

The Test of a Man: Being the Purusha-Paiksha of Vidyapati Thakkura by G.A. Grierson, The Royal Asiatic Society, London 1935.

Love Songs of Vidyapati Translated by Pralay Bhattacharya, Sterling Publishers, 1998. ('100 erotic songs').

Man in Indian Tradition: Vidyapati's Discourse on Purusa by Hetukar Jha, Aryan Book International, New Delhi, 2002.

Minstrels of God Part 2 by Bankey Behari, Bharatiya Vidya Bhavan, Bombay, 1970. [Pages 246-52].
Wikipedia article.

Slokas...

[Krishna about Radha]

Her childhood and youth have come together...

her eyes have given way to what she does hear;

and, her speech is clever and her laugh is deep,

it was as if over this earth moon rays did seep.

She takes up a mirror to herself be arranging...

she asks, "The game of love is what, playing?"

Many times she looks at her breasts, secretly,

and is smiling to see them rounding perfectly!

At first, they were like plums, oranges... now;

daily from love, her limbs are blossoming now.

O Krishna, I saw a girl who was so beautiful;

in her, childhood and youth were, wonderful.

And Vidyapati says, "O maid, most foolish...

the wise would say, both you do accomplish."

Why was that moon-face one my path crossing?
Just for a moment, her eyes, mine were meeting!
That one's sideways glance was all too ardent...
That day for me may turn out as a bad portent!
My thoughts were set upon those breasts of her:
love lay waking in my heart... to there discover.
That voice of hers was then in my ears ringing:
I would have gone... but my feet were refusing.
The bonds of hope they're still constraining me!
Vidyapati: "Love is a tide, pulling constantly!"

This is O such a joyful day for me:
bathing, I saw my love completely!
From her hair, a stream of water...
clouds, strings of pearls, a shower!
She, did wipe her face so intensely
like cleaning a golden mirror to see
and to discover both of her breasts
where once were gold cups as rests:
then, let her intimate place be seen!
Vidyapati: "No more, to be seen!"

On seeing me lurking she smiled slightly,

as if the moon the night lit up... brightly!

When sidelong glances on me she rained,

a swarm of bees all of the heavens filled.

Who knows who to that girl is belonging,

who makes heart shake, then is leaving?

In lotus-flower of love bee is imprisoned,

to see that shy one passing I was amazed.

Then her breasts' beauty I did remember:

golden lily every heart did snare, forever!

That one was half-hidden, half-revealed:

her rounded breasts told me she desired!

Vidyapati says, "That, was Love's dawn:

does Love's secret arrow spare any born?"

Wherever both of her feet may be falling

both of them a lotus-flower is uplifting!

Wherever her body swaying passes by,

it is like waves of lightning, in the sky!

Beyond any radiance was what I saw...

she now sits in my heart, for evermore!

Wherever she may open her eyes upon,

I can now see water-lilies, thereupon!

Wherever her light laughter is ringing,

from envy any nectar near, is souring!
Wherever her sidelong glance may fall
the myriads of Love's arrows will fall!
Even to see such beauty for a moment
is enough to three worlds circumvent!
O if only one more time I can see her,
then this mourning will... disappear!
Vidyapati says, "The truth's this: for
Your dear sake, I'll be bringing her!"

[Radha about Krishna]

O my dear, how can I describe Krishna's beauty?
That dream-like form who can describe properly?
That beautiful body of His is as fresh as a cloud,
that yellow costume is a lightning-flash, proud!
His hair flowing in waves is black, O so black!
Peacock's plume is near moon's orb, to attack!
For that fragrance of the tall pine and jasmine
Love dismayed shoots flower-arrows... a sign!
Vidyapati asks, "What more, is there to say?
treasury of Love Nature has emptied today!"

Krishna I was desiring so much to be seeing,
but when I did with fear my heart was filling.
Since that time I am full of love and foolish,
I don't know what to say, do, what to wish?
These two eyes are weeping like raindrops,
going pit-a-pat my heart is, it never stops.
I can't think why I looked at Him, my dear:
for a whim my life into His, did disappear!
I can't tell what that dear thief did to me...
when I saw Him he stole my heart, left me!
As He went many signs of love He showed:
better if I forget, but they are remembered!
Vidyapati says, "Listen, O lovely maiden:
heart have patience, he will come, again!"

My dear, how can I tell how much I'm grieving?
That flute, poison through my body is blowing!
I keep hearing going on and on the sound of it...
then heart and body in shame melts, bit by bit!
In that supreme moment my body overflows...
I do not dare to lift my eyes, so another knows.
With elders, such emotion sweeps through me

that my dress I pull to hide each limb carefully.
I walk around the house, stepping silently I go:
my secret shame kind fate has hidden, I know:
rapture fills my heart and body, my girdle slips!
Vidyapati is dazed! What can come to his lips!

Friend, what can I say? It's a shame to be telling
all my Lover did... whether or not I was willing.
I, just a young thing, in love's ways unlearned...
messenger took me to Him, away I never turned.
When I saw that one my body began to shiver...
He was so fierce to take me, now and not never!
As He embraced me my mind suddenly left me:
could I tell the love-games He played with me?
In everything he did my Lord was not gentle...
can I talk about it with friends, of it can I tell?
Do not ask about it, you know it well enough?
That girl is happy who He doesn't treat rough.
Vidyapati says, "Do not any fear be having...
such is the first-time the way of love-making!"

Dear friend, do not urge me, me do not be urging;
what can I do, if my fears that one was soothing?

My years are few and I'm not as old as Krishna:
I become ashamed quickly, I'm much too tender!
That Lord so cruel with me played, impatiently;
can I tell how many woes that night fell on me?
Passion overcame me and my mind I was losing:
when that one broke my girdle I'm not knowing!
He pinned down my arms and held me closely...
and then, this heart of mine was beating wildly.
I allowed that one to see my eyes, streaming...
but, even after that, Krishna was not pitying!
These lips were parched by my wicked lover...
with night's help Rahu* of moon was devourer!
With His nails, He was tearing my breasts...
like a lion tears at an elephant, or other beasts.
Vidyapati says, "O you woman, full of love...
you knew well Krishna was on fire with love!"

*Note: Rahu in Hindu tradition is a demon snake.

CHANDIDAS (1417-1477). Chandidas was a Vaishnavite poet/saint of the fourteenth century. Born into a Brahmin family he belonged to a society ridden with religious bigotry and strong Brahminical authoritarianism. Though he was the disciple of a Brahmin priest who believed in harsh and ascetic principles, Chandidas's love for poetry inevitably came in the way of his religious devotion.

He spent hours near the river, where Rami, the washerman's daughter, came to wash clothes. Rami was the daughter of a low-caste was also a young widow and barred on both counts from any social intercourse with a man such as Chandidas. But, she had a divine voice and held no fear. Chandidas would listen to her songs for hours. Rami was aware of the young Brahmin's interest and was a great admirer of his poetry. They were drawn to each other. Their romance became a major scandal. Though the strength of Rami's personality sustained Chandidas for awhile against the attacks of the Brahmins, he was still in awe of the temple priest whose overpowering hold finally led to his denouncing Rami and agreeing to perform a religious ceremony in the temple to repent for his sins.

Rami, refusing to believe that Chandidas would actually disown her, battled to reach the temple on time. Distraught and bleeding she confronted Chandidas in the presence of his religious mentor. Chandidas, believing in a more just and loving God in place of the harsh divinity offered by the priest of the temple, renounced his religious bindings, dissociated himself from the orthodox Brahminical order and left the village with Rami.

Over 1250 of his poems relate to his love of Rami and the love of Radha and Krishna in Bengali. Chandidas gives the yearning of Radha a distinctly Bengali rendition and in the process captures much of the social conditions of the day. The 412 songs in the *Srikrishsnakirtana* are divided into thirteen sections representing the core of the Radha-Krishna legendary cycle with variants providing excellent comparative material. Bankey Behari states that Vidyapati and Chandidas knew each other... obviously Vidyapati influencing the younger poet.

Further Reading...

Love Songs of Chandidas: Rebel Poet-Priest of Bengal, Translated by Deban Bhattacharya, Grove, New York, 1970.
Chandidas Padavali by Chandidas, Human Touch Publishing, Key Biscayne, 1901. (Reprint).
The Story of Chandidas: A Poetic Representation of the Fusion of Sakta and Vaishnava Cultures, by Priyaranjan Sen, Indian Publications, Calcutta, 1963.
Chandidas by S. Sen, Sahitya Akademi, New Delhi 1971.
Minstrels of God Part 2 by Bankey Behari, Bharatiya Vidya Bhavan, Bombay, 1970. (Pages 234-245).
Wikipedia article.

Slokas...

[Rami about Chandidas]

Lost in contemplation, enjoyment of the Divine play,
you roam the forest: I miss your face, I grieve all day.
Like an age is just a moment's separation from you...
I suffer us being apart, heart is restless, mind is too!
Your lovely hair I see, your face's sparkling beauty...
I wish I had no eyelashes, so you I could always see!
I am the one with no luck and my lot I'm lamenting:
I'm yours, you are mine, no other mine I am calling.
Rami who's grief-stricken, O Chandidas, says this:
"For me when apart, world only full of darkness is."

[Chandidas about Rami]

O washerman's daughter Rami, I surrender to your
small lotus-feet... they have cooled my heart before!
Goddess of knowledge, Lord's consort, eyes light...

I worship you, songs of praise... my garlands bright.

Like washerman from Radha's time you do not lust;

Chandidas sings: his love for Rami's like gold-dust!

[Radha about Krishna]

Who sang to me the Lord's name of Krishna, O so sweet?

It fell on my ears like balm, yet Him I'm restless to meet!

Nectar making His name I can't measure, it's on my lips

always... the more I say it I pass away, taking joyful sips.

What other name is there that is possessing such power?

Does any ecstasy exist, that His touch will not shower?

I don't care about anything else, I give up all propriety...

I rush to meet that One and turn my back on all society!

I am completely helpless and no matter how hard I try...

I'm powerless to control my mind, it after Him does fly!

Chandidas... "He demolishes society's fortress holding

us and demands all beauty in us to Him we be offering!"

O my friend, the dark waters remind me of my Krishna:

all dreams and when awake my mind sees only Krishna!

When I comb my dark curls to dry them they remind me

of Him so I hesitate to put collyrium in my eyes suddenly.

O friend, how will time go without Krishna's company?

Ah, there is pain in my heart I must hold back, secretly!
Beauty of Krishna's form pierced my heart like an arrow:
Chandidas offers: "What hurts in, out doesn't show?"
Krishna is my shelter, of all He is the essence... and
that Krishna's my life's breath, He is neck's garland.
Krishna is that pearl that from my nose is hanging...
Krishna is the beautiful blue *sari* I am now wearing.
Krishna has taken over both my soul and my body...
a maid-servant of His I've become, I say it honestly.
Krishna is my strength and Krishna is my witness...
Krishna is all my riches and Krishna is all I possess.
It was my good luck the Creator, Krishna gave me:
even cuckoo rejoices seeing Krishna embracing me!
Chandidas is saying this, "Radha keeps on keeping
Krishna like a garland on her breast, there residing."

O Beloved, You're asking me to tell my story to You:
since childhood Your love made me a victim... of You.
Even at that tender age it wouldn't let me be peaceful:
tortured, I've decided to die with a mind of You, full!
Then I can be born once again, next time as Krishna...
and You, O my Beloved, can be born again as Radha.
Then I'll be make love to You and when You're caught

I will stand under the *kadamba* tree, playing the flute.
And when You go crazy and rush to me I'll disappear:
then You'll know separation's grief. Chandidas hear!

O my Beloved, how can I reveal to You my suffering?
To You in life and in death I am totally surrendering!
With arrow of Your Love, my heart has been pierced:
offering all at Your feet, I You, as a servant, served...
because I knew in all three worlds none would call me
by my name, Radha, and stay there waiting upon me.
Where to now go as not on this bank nor on the other
is there another... whom I can call my Beloved lover!
Your lotus-feet comfort the afflicted... I shelter there:
  it is not right to throw me away, without a prayer!
Darling, think about this, where else can I be going?
If I don't see You for a moment, life is heavy-going!
"Radha says, she wants Krishna like a garland tied
around her heart," Chandidas is singing unbridled.

Beloved, O my life, I've offered my mind, soul, body:
all the world and society holds sacred I offer, totally!
Dear, aren't You Lord of universe, Who *yogis* adore?
We, are just a *gopi*, are we wise... how do we adore?

Drowning mind, body, heart in Love we at Your feet
offer all; life's goal, You, we only see, want to meet!
I don't care about disgrace, if the world says I'm evil:
such scorn as that I'll value and the pain I'll not feel!
You know me totally, I am faithful to You, always...
at Your feet Radha gives her all... Chandidas says.

His Love, what pain comes to the heart from it?
I will go where His Love is unknown, escape It!
I wooed His Love with smiles, now in tears I go:
mind of high caste loving Him, pain will know!
My pain, is like the lotus hit by storm of hail...
unhappy me, victim of pain, at separation pale!
This, is said by Chandidas... "That condition
of that helpless one due to Love, I write upon."

That love of His, in heart causes great suffering...
I'll travel to where His Love they're not knowing.
I wooed His Love with smiles, now... I only cry:
any high-born girl loving Him will be left to sigh!
My pain could a lotus struck by hail be likened...
now, pained, unhappy me, cries as we are parted!
Chandidas has now revealed... that her helpless

state is a sickness His Love brings: more or less!

O my dear friend, a great secret I will reveal to you...
in heaven's name, the word 'Love', don't take to you.
Not for a moment look upon Love's manifestation...
when that word is said, shut ear without hesitation!
The city of Love leave... stay in the forest far away,
so... if 'Love' you hear, if you wait it does not stay.
This, is the sad state Love has now brought me to...
it is so hard to take its pain! Chandidas cannot too!

My condition is hopeless, another's will enslaves me:
it's O so painful that in my movements I am not free!
I'm unlucky since the Creator wrote on my forehead...
now the sea of nectar is like poison, for on it I am fed!
When to cool heat of breasts a cold stone I embraced,
it changed into a fiery coal... into ashes I was burned!
To have shade under the trees I went... I stood alone:
instantly the leaves were flames, I was caught, gone!
Then into the Jamuna I dived , its cool waters to take:
it suddenly became so hot my skin scalded, did flake!
Why should I go on living, I should take poison or die.

Chandidas: "To know God's ways is hard, but try!"

I will live in Love's land and build a house of Love...
Love will be my only friend, my neighbour I'll Love.
The rafters will be made of Love and the doors too...
I'll pass time in Love, in hope of Love I'll live... too!
I will lie on Love's bed, in Love's covers wrapped...
in Love, goodbye boredom, my ears to Love turned!
In Love's waters, Love's collyrium to eye I'll apply:
Love is my religion, my life for Love I'm sacrificing!
I'll put Love's ring in my nose, watch it with eyes:
Love's collyrium, will be there... Chandidas says.

[Krishna about Radha]

The day dawns, and on my lips is her name: Radha!
She's My heart's garland, I lie down I remember her!
I worship Radha, and her name I am remembering...
and I'm doing this for love of that one to be winning.
I think of her on my bed, in dreams she is with Me...
I think of her when I eat, when I rest she's with Me!
At times with flute in hand and often when it I play

I roam forest saying her name, to win her love I play!

With a full heart, I surrender at lotus-feet of Radha!

O you seekers of Love take comfort at feet of Radha!

Follow my advice, bow to her and if for many a year

you worship Me and not her too, it's fruitless, hear?

Tears sprang from Krishna's eyes and He obtained

Radha's embrace, lucky One! Chandidas explained.

KABIR (1440-1518). Kabir (meaning 'great') was born near Varanasi (Banaras), India. He was brought up by an elderly Muslim weaver-couple named Niru and Nirna, having been abandoned shortly after birth. He learnt the same trade as his new parents and used the imagery of weaving often in his poems.

Kabir is not easily categorised as a Sufi or a Yogi as he is all of these. He is revered by Muslims, Hindus and Sikhs. He stands as a unique, saintly, yet very human, bridge between the great traditions that live in India. Kabir says of himself that he is, "at once the child of Allah and Ram."

It is said that he had a number of Gurus or spiritually perfected Masters. One was a Sufi Master named Sheikh Taqqi. The most famous was Ramanand. Kabir wanted to become his disciple, but it was said that Ramanand only accepted Brahmins as disciples. Kabir refused to accept this. He devised a plan! One day he hid under the steps of the *ghats* where Ramanand would go to bathe early every morning. Ramanand stepped on the body of Kabir (as Kabir had hoped). The Master having trod on one of God's creatures called out

"Ram, Ram", his personal mantra or prayer to God. Kabir, having obtained the prayer began to recite it and Ramanand on seeing the sincerity and cleverness of the young man accepted him as a disciple.

Kabir strongly denounced the orthodox ways of religions: rituals and ceremonies. His quick wit and razor sharp tongue tore strips off the hypocritical theologians and priests.

He proved to the people through the pure logic of the heart the stupidity of believing that religions are different from each other by pointing out the essential sameness in all of them.

At a time when the Muslims and Hindus were at each other's throats this was a very brave thing to do, and by doing it he brought an end to their fighting. After many years his Master gave him the experience of God-consciousness and perfected him. Kabir became a Perfect Master or Sadguru himself... experiencing being God and man simultaneously.

In many of his poems he tells of this experience and teaches us that we too are inwardly God and have only to pray to God, follow a True Master, love our fellow creatures and above all, be honest, to experience this same Self in all of us.

Kabir's short teaching poems or couplets *dohas* which are called *sakhis* (meaning 'sayings' or 'witness') are like short, hard, sharp punches at the heart – direct, full of power, they take your breath away for a moment, you see stars, they hurt for quite some time afterwards, they are a real shock to the system, to the intellect, the dishonesty we nurture inside ourselves.

Further Reading...

Seven Hundred Sayings of Kabir, Translation & Introduction by Paul Smith. New Humanity Books, Melbourne, 1988. New Humanity Books Campbells Creek, 2005, 2012.
Kabir: Translated from Original Hindi into English by S.H. Jhabvala, Bombay (date?)
A Translation of Kabir's complete Bijak into English by Prem Chand, Calcutta, 1911.
Kabir: The Weaver in God's Name. V.K. Sethi, Radha Soami Satsang Beas, Amritsar. 1984.
The Bijak of Kabir by Ahmed Shah, Hamipur, 1917 Reprint: Asian Publication Services, New Delhi 1977.
The Adi-Granth London, E. Trumpp 1877. (Trumpp's translation includes some of Kabir's poems.)
One Hundred Poems of Kabir. Rabindratnath Tagore, with an Introduction by E. Underhill, London, 1914.
Kabir. Charlotte Vaudeville, Oxford, 1974.
Sufis, Mystics and Yogis of India Bankey Behari, ed. K.M. Munshi, Bombay, Bharatiya Vidya Bhavan, 1962. (Trans. of Kabir's poems: pages 221-252.)
A Weaver Named Kabir... Selected Verses. Charlotte Vaudeville, Oxford India 1993.
The Bijak of Kabir. Linda Hess and Shukdev Singh. North Point Press, San Francisco. 1983.
Kabir: The Apostle of Hindu-Muslim Unity. Muhammad Hedayetullah. M. Banarsidass. Delhi 1977.

1008 Kabir Vani: Nectar of Truth and Knowledge. 'Kunwar'
Anil Kumar [Translator]. Manoj Pub. Delhi 2005.
Sakhis...

The nearest relative one has is the Master:

awakening of spirit is a gift... none greater.

No greater giver of Gifts exists than Hari,*

His servants haven't equal in a community.

*Note: Hari = God.

Sixty-four large lamps may be burning bright

and fourteen moons inside might give light,

but moonlight won't exist in the slightest

where Perfect Master finds no home to rest.

Darkness of night was meant to be abolished

by eighty-four hundred million moons passed:

but without the true Guru* they came, went,

still blind... though many lives they spent!

*Note: Guru: Kabir often talks of true Masters and false masters. The
Master or Guru is the God-realized human being... the true Teacher as
with Ramanand, Kabir, John the Baptist, Francis of Assisi, Hafiz, Rumi,
Ramakrishna, etc.

If the so called 'guru' cannot see well then
his disciple is blind from birth... and when
those who are blind lead those who are blind
and both in a hole fall, both you won't find.

Let the Perfect Master burn everything away
using Wisdom as tool: let Guru have his way;
with the Word as scraper let him be scraping
and let soul be a mirror from his polishing.

The true Hero is really the Perfect Master,
who let fly arrow, a Word: the Great Archer.
I fell on the dirt as soon as target was hit,
and a deep wound opened after receiving it.

I was saved when I was about to be drowned
by whim of Guru, by whose wave I surfed:
I witnessed the old form, the boat, shatter,
and I was saved when of 'me' I jumped clear.

Stability and salvation were found by me
when the Guru set me in the Source, firmly:
Kabir, the Diamond of Reality can be bought
on bank of Lake Mansarover* if It, is sought.

*Note: A lake at the foot of Kailas peak. Lake of the Mind.

I could no longer speak and I was senseless
and my ears could no longer hear, I confess;
for legs to move was no longer a possibility
when arrow of the Master deeply pierced me

Infinite is the Glory of the Perfect Master
and also his Grace, for he's the great Giver;
eyes were opened to Infinity by his Grace
and I then saw beyond all time and space.

I was slowly following in the world's wake
and following Vedic rites, for their sake...
then on the path the Perfect Master met me
and in my hand he put a lamp so I could see.

Lamp full of oil to me the true Guru gave,
its wick won't dry up, oil one needn't save:
as far as I feel, all bartering is finished…
no longer I'll go to world to be replenished.

You have found the Master: but what then
if your mind's still full of mistakes? When
cloth has been soiled and spoiled already,
coming to poor red dye what fate shall be?

Myself to Perfect Master I've offered again,
with all the sincerity my heart can contain:
this, the Age of Death, vainly attacked me
because my determination went on endlessly.

The Perfect Master placed bow in his hand
and let fly his arrows at where I did stand,
one arrow which with his Love he had fired
wounded me ceaselessly: my heart pierced.

No longer able to laugh… or to talk at all,
changeable mind is finished, beyond recall!
Kabir says that it often stabbed me through,
that sharp weapon, that Word of the Guru.

The Perfect Guru fits arrow then lets fly,
he keeps arm steady with his watchful eye:
my Guru's arrow did hit my poor naked form
and the Forest burst into a blazing storm.

Kabir, when the Perfect Master I've found,
salt vanished, into the flour it was ground:
disappeared have caste, lineage and family,
and so what name then can you give to me?

Finding Guru is the greatest benefit for you,
alone you are lost, I Kabir, say this is true.
It's like a moth that's drawn to lamp's fire,
it knows its fate… and it falls to its desire.

Maya* is like the lamp and the moth is man;
circling it, man falls… won't stop if he can.
Kabir says, it's only due to wisdom of Guru
that some are saved from Maya, though few.

*Note: Illusion, false attachment. Ignorance. God's shadow.

Seated on platform of Divine Consciousness
the Master gave to me the gift of firmness:
now, being liberated from all doubt and fear,
the only One Who Exists is adored by Kabir.

Kabir, they haven't found the Perfect Master
and only know half, remain none the wiser:
dressed in robes of the wandering ascetic,
door to door they beg, they are so pathetic.

Perfect Master is my Hero: Kabir's no liar!
Like blacksmith, he keeps iron in the fire:
he made it pure and into gold he made it,
its essence he extracted by the fire he lit.

With patience, consistency, Guru gave me
that everlasting Treasure of the Reality:
many farmers would like a crop like this,
but Kabir won't share It, for It is now his.

At intersection is laid out the dice-board
in market that goes up, down: none scored.
When you have as your partner the Master,
it's impossible in this game to be the loser.

By his taking up the dice that's called Love,
by making the board from his bodily glove,
learning from the Master all about the throw
servant Kabir played from the first "go".

When I had found Grace with the True Guru
to me he made a revelation unique and true,
then poured out upon me the cloud of Love
and my body was fully soaked from up above.

When the snake of separation is in the body

no ritual word can control or set it free:

whoever's separated from Ram* won't survive

but if he survives, he will be mad... if alive.

The body was entered by snake of separation

and the heart felt its fangs of separation...

yes, not one movement the snake does make,

saying: "Bite as you like, more I can take."

In sky, Kunjha cranes make mournful cries:

thunder is heard, lakes fill from the skies,

but one who has been deserted by her Lord

suffers torment that can't be told by word.

Midnight the Lakvi bird is alone, agitated,

at day's break she and her mate are united;

but ones who from Ram are always distant,

not day nor night is He found for an instant.

In separation from Ocean (the Pearl Giver)
oh conch shell wait, don't yet be lamenter;
you will have to cry out in all the shrines
when the Sun rises and upon you it shines.

Inside the heart there burns a large fire...
yet no smoke is seen, but fire grows higher:
he who it burns away that flame does know,
and he also knows He Who did make it grow.

In the fires of separation the log that's wet
smoulders, smokes and spits where it's set:
from separation it will never find a way out
until it becomes ashes: that, do not doubt.

After death comes please don't let us meet
O Ram, this Kabir prays: a prayer complete!
When into dust becomes that old rusted iron,
what can be done by Philosopher's Stone?

He will surely die, that one who is wounded,

even if the knife of separation is blunted:

he then lies down under the tree, moaning;

will it be today or tomorrow he'll be dying?

Physician, go home and look after yourself,

you can do nothing, so see to your health:

the One causing disease that hurts so much,

only He can cure disease, His Grace is such.

Do not heap abuse upon that separated one,

for that one is a King, though in a dungeon.

A body that doesn't feel pangs of separation

stays forever a place for fiery annihilation.

Body is the lute and veins are the strings,

separation plays endlessly on both and sings;

but this music can be heard by not anyone,

only by the soul and God, the Supreme One.

I've been waiting, waiting for so many days
Ram, I've searched the road and the ways:
to meet You my heart is longing, is longing,
still there is no peace my soul is knowing.

Away my great despair will never be going
if it is only a message that I am hearing,
it will only leave when Hari comes to me
or when I am finally allowed to go to Hari.

I will burn away this form of mine to ashes
so that to the sky much smoke then rises:
isn't it possible that then Hari will pity
me and quench that fire will rain on me.

These eyes have become completely insane
because they desire to see You again, again:
I didn't find You and I didn't find happiness
and all I have gained is despair in excess.

That One Who is the One that one is loving

will one way or another, closer be coming:

from that One to Whom one gave body, soul,

on trust, impossible to part: part or whole!

Only one mind exists for disciple and Master

for mind's merged with Mind: praise merger!

Master is not happy if cleverness is shown,

only if sincerity in the disciple has grown.

On the path stands the lonely wife, waiting,

suddenly she runs to the traveller, asking:

"Tell me, give me some news of my Husband,*

when will He come, return to this land?"

*Note: God or the Perfect Master.

It's surely impossible for me to come to You

and to make You come here is impossible too:

You'll take my life away from me this way,

burning it all away in separation all day.

Kabir, I am suffering deeply, so completely
that from this cage, pain is never set free:
this agony of love, unlike anything at all,
into core of my being cut, past every wall.

Wound that separation causes is so complete
that total destruction the body does meet:
the One Who strikes, alone knows suffering;
except for one who suffering is enduring.

Kabir, day went by while she was waiting
and the night has slowly away been passing:
one who is separated does not her Lord meet
but spends her life in torment and defeat.

Let that one who is separated pass away
or else reveal Yourself to that one today!
This burning that seems to go on forever
is impossible for Kabir to bear any longer.

The body and soul were burnt to extinction
in that great blazing inferno of separation:
the suffering is no longer felt by the dead,
it is only that Fire that by that pain is fed.

Good qualities of my Lord beyond counting,
in my heart are written in large lettering:
to drink some water now I would not dare,
I'm frightened they'd wash away from there.

Kabir, either that one love has never tasted
or, after, its flavour he has not enjoyed:
like one visiting a house, finding emptiness
leaves it, being unchanged: not more or less.

Within my eyes come, so I then may gaze
upon You all through the nights and days.
Let it soon be that the day will come to me
when sight of Him is given by great Hari!

The tears of people who are wicked appear
like the good people who shed many a tear:
when tears of blood are streaming from eyes
then know in that heart Love certainly lies.

Disciple was burnt by fire the Guru started;
   that one was burnt in fire separation fed:
that bundle that was a piece of grass today
was saved when it embraced the pile of hay.

The fire was lit and the water was aflame,
the gigantic blaze leapt from where it came:
   the river that had run now remained still,
no water flowed for the fish to have its fill.

The crimson cloud pressed upon the terrain,
   hot fiery coals everywhere began to rain:
   Kabir says that such a great fire did grow
that all the world was scorched in one blow.

On the ocean the great fire raged unchecked
and to burning cinders the river was changed:
when he woke up Kabir looked and did see
that the fish had climbed up onto the tree.

That arrow which yesterday You fired at me
has now become something I treasure dearly:
with arrow You shot yesterday hit me today,
as I can't find Truth unless it comes my way.

Kabir, what are you doing, always sleeping?
Wake and get up and your fate be lamenting
That one lying in the grave that is silent,
can he happily sleep when his life is spent?

Kabir, what are you doing always sleeping?
Please wake and the great Lord be adoring!
You'll be made to fall asleep in another way
then your legs will be stretched out all day.

Call out, keep calling for God Who is great,
and refuse to make endless sleep your fate:
if you loudly cry your woes, night and day,
in the end He will certainly listen your way.

Kabir, it isn't an easy thing for one to do,
to call upon Name of Great God to help you;
when one juggles above the stake the cost
is that if one slips and falls then he's lost.

Through his previous mistakes and evil ways
man picked up poison that on his head stays
but millions of actions are annihilated
instantly, if God he trusts and is protected.

Instantly millions of actions are wiped out
by calling on the Name; that, don't doubt:
good deeds that for ages have accumulated
will lead nowhere, unless Name is invoked.

Kabir, the essence can be found in Prayer,
and a snare is everything else that's there
in the world, which I've searched end to end:
all else is Death, unless that Name is invoked.

Kabir, what are you doing, always sleeping?
Why don't you stand up and begin searching?
The One from Whom you are now so far away
become united with again, so Kabir does say.

The God that the man has desired to obtain
is the God that he will obtain: that's plain.
Great thirst is not quenched by drop of dew
unless water is carried all the way through.

Kabir, when the mind was sparked off again
fire was all over, so difficult to constrain.
Take hold of the bucket of Prayer, quickly
rush and douse fire that burns so fiercely.

Man didn't question the One Who did know,

so off he went like fools who stupidity sow.

If the blind meet only those who are blind

then who'll help them the true road to find?

Kabir, the fragrance of the Sandalwood tree

permeates trees growing in jungle uselessly:

it has changed all that was in its vicinity,

and into something like itself, undoubtedly.

The holiness of the Saint*is retained by him

in the middle of all those who commit sin,

like Sandalwood tree that cool does remain

even in poisonous snake's embrace, a chain.

*Note: Sometimes Kabir talks about true Saints (God-advanced souls) and
sometimes false saints.

Many horses and line of elephants marching,

canopies with royal insignia, flags fluttering:

being beggar is better than such prosperity,

if beggar spends days calling Ram constantly.

Kabir says, I have two companions with me,
Ram is one and the other's the Saint to see:
one of them brings to me eternal salvation,
other makes me take the Name as invocation.

Those whose understanding counts as nothing
can have undisturbed sleep when sleeping;
but when out from my ignorance I did wake,
great was the problem that I did undertake.

Oh Kabir, to Kaaba I was journeying one day
when suddenly God stood, blocking my way;
the Lord then put following question to me:
"Who was it told you Kaaba to go and see?"

A closet or a room is not filled with rubies
and the Hamsa bird in a line never flies;
you'll not find lions hunting in big groups
and Saints never walk together in troops.

Kabir, that day is truly a very blessed day
when those Saints happen to come your way!
Take them closely into your embrace and all
of your sins away from you will then fall.

You should not be measuring their holiness
by sweetness of the words they may express:
they'll show bottom to give assurance to you
then out into the deep they will take you.

A death neverending is life of the devotee,
living like a lord is the man of stupidity:
the stupid man cannot tell right from wrong,
his aim is to fill his belly all day long.

O Kabir, the Ocean's waves continue to roll
and roll in and out in this gigantic bowl!
To God's devotee I give myself as sacrifice:
to he who diving now, again in Ocean lies.

God's lover is like a cloth that's priceless,

yet devotee can't be soiled, become a mess;

but goddess of senses idolater is a black rag:

used whenever one wants it is its price, tag.

My Lord in all forms that exist is living,

there is no seat where He is not sitting:

yet, true married bliss is for that one

in whom He is shining as the Glorious Sun.

NANAK (1469-1539). He was born at Rai-Bhoi-di Talwandi in the present district of Shekhupura (Pakistan), now Nanakana Sahib. His father, Mehta Kalyan Das, was the agent and Chief Accountant of Rai Bular. His mother was Mata Tripta, a simple, pious and extremely religious woman. Nanak had an elder sister, Nanki, who always cherished her younger brother.

Nanak was an extraordinary and different child in many ways. At seven he learnt Hindi and Sanskrit. He surprised his teachers with the sublimity of his knowledge about divine things. At the age of 13 he learned Persian and at 16 he was the most learned young man in the region. He was married to Mata Sulakhni, who gave birth to two sons: Sri Chand and Lakhmi Das. In November 1504 his elder sister Nanaki took him to Sultanpurlodhi where her husband Jai Ram got him the position of storekeeper in the Modikhana of the local Nawab, Daulat Khan Lodhi.

At 38 he heard God's call to dedicate himself to the service of humanity after bathing in a river near Sultanpur Lodhi. The very first sentence that he said then was, 'There is no Hindu, no Muslim'. It is said that one of his Guru's was the great Kabir (see his section previously) who he is said to have met when young and whose poems appear with Ramdas', Namdev's and other *Bhakti* poets in the Sikh bible, *The Adi Granth.*

He undertook long travels to preach his unique and divine doctrine (Sikhism). After visiting different places in the Punjab he went on four long tours covering different Hindu and Buddhist religious places in India and abroad including Tibet. He went to Mecca, Medina, Baghdad, Peshwar, Syria, Turkey and Persia.

The real aim of this tour was awakening the people to realize the truth about God and to introduce Sikhism. He established a network of preaching centres of Sikhism which were called 'Manjis'. He appointed able and committed followers as its head (preacher of Sikhism). The seeds of Sikhism were sown all over India and abroad in well-planned manner.

In the year 1520, Babar attacked India. His troops slaughtered thousands of innocent civilians of all walks of life. Women and children were made captives and all their property looted at Amiabad. Nanak challenged this act of barbarity in strong words. He was arrested and released, shortly after Babar realized his blunder. All the prisoners were released.

He settled down at Kartarpur city which was founded by

him in 1522 and spent the rest of his life there.

He rejected the path of renunciation or Yoga, the authority of the *Vedas* and the Hindu caste system. He emphasized the leading of householder's life, unattached to gross materialism. He preached the idea of God as Supreme, Universal, All-powerful and truthful. As a social reformer he upheld the cause of women, downtrodden and the poor.

He was a born poet. He wrote 947 poems. He was also a musician and with the company of Bhai Mardana composed tunes in various Indian classical *ragas*.

Further Reading...

The Adi Granth or The Holy Scriptures of the Sikhs, Translated from the original Gurumukhi with introductory essays by Ernest Trumpp, Munshiram Manoharlal, Pvt. Ltd. New Delhi, 2010. Originally published in 1877.
Hymns of Guru Nanak, Translated by Khushwant Singh, Sangam Books, Bombay, 1978.
Indian Mystic Verse, Translated by Hari Prasad Shastri, Shanti Sadan, London, 1941. (Pages 70-77).
Guru Nanak (India: National Biography Series) by Dr. Gopal Singh, National Book Trust, new Delhi, 1984.
The Philosophy of Guru Nanak by Ishar Singh, India Publications Bureau, Panjab University, Chandigarth, 1969.
Travels of Guru Nanak, by Ishar Singh, India Publications Bureau, Panjab University, Chandigarth, 1978.
Sufis, Mystics and Yogis of India by Bankey Behari, Bombay, Bharatiya Vidya Bhavan, 1962. (Pages 208-221).

Slokas…

The mind is circled by desires, work of desires is doing:
those ignorant who worship duality God is punishing.
If one worship the Self, nothing occurs without Guru;
silent prayers, austerity, all is by the will of the Guru.
Through destiny all falls into your lap, this is said by
Nanak… for accepted is who to please Him does try!

Whose minds lust are wrong, will their hearts see it?
Lustful-minded are One but not, their lot isn't yet lt!
Inner devotion and action work, it is true, not a toy…
Word as touchstone disciple uses to… mind destroy!
With mind is a quarrel, with Mind is reconciliation…
what heart desires it has by Guru's word's initiation.
Name's nectar is enjoyed by whose actions are pure,
who fights with all but mind wastes a life… for sure.
But, who through the Guru to God does be devoted
Nanak, is true as Guru's helper: mind's imprisoned.

Every one is Yours, You belong to every one…
You're the all Who is worthwhile, in each one.

To You we're continually begging and praying:
we go on asking You for You, we go on asking!
Whoever You give to will everything obtain...
from some You are far, for others easy to gain.
Without You is no where for one to be asking:
it is best one's mind, this... is clearly knowing.
Whether they know it or not, all praise You...
at Your gate, Your disciples You let see You!

That one who into court of God is admitted,
is in every court in this and the next world...
and that one's honoured wherever he may go,
each sinner who sees his face is saved: it's so!
The treasure of the Name is inside that one:
so much exalted by His Name... is that one.
The Name should be worshipped, treasured:
and every sin by that Name will be removed.
One's mind that concentrates on the Name,
in the world they are strong due to the Name.

The scholar explains the *Vedas* by reading and writing,
but infatuation with the Illusion him to sleep is lulling.
The Name of God is forgotten, by love his of duality...

such a heart that's foolish will be punished, eventually.
He never thinks of Who gave to him the body and soul:
he never thinks of Who each day his bread does control.
Noose of Death from his neck hasn't yet been severed,
he keeps coming back here and going again, unlearned!
This blind and lustful one isn't a thing seeing, nothing:
what's been written down before for him he is earning!
A true Guru by a fulfilled destiny is finally discovered,
Name that gives comfort comes and in heart is lodged.
That one will enjoy comfort like clothes that are put on:
all of the time will pass in comfort, it will go on and on!
May that Name never be by Nanak's mind forgotten...
for by that at Truth's gate he'll gain the brightest One.

I'm God's musician, the Lord and Master,
to the gate of God I have come... a player.
in this house God has heard my singing...
to mouth this instrument... He is placing!
God, having called this musician asked...
"What was the reason, you were coming?"
"O merciful Lord, give gift lasting forever:
I meditate on Your Name over and over!"
God gave to me say His Name silently...

He has dressed Nanak in coat of divinity.
Bhajans...

Remember God continually, Him in the mind staying:
be with Saints not lust's path... His Name be taking!
Those remembering the Lord, to hell are never going...
hot wind won't touch he, who in heart He is residing!
They're beautiful, shining, any sitting with the pious:
who ever collects His wealth, are deep, neverending.
Who, by nectar of God is intoxicated... upon seeing
such a face and life, at Guru's feet are worshipping.
Whoever God makes His own, the Lord is knowing;
is a hero, the first, on that forehead is much writing!
That one who heart in her Lord has been drowning,
she enjoys much, sins not, crosses over, is working;
Creator lives in her heart, her life's fruit is having,
her Husband in her heart is, a marriage... lasting.
Immortality is obtained by who the fear-destroying
One saves. Nanak: in His hem we over are going!

O Lord, no longer can I live, separated from You,
I survive by singing praises of the deeds You do.
Gone are nights of remembering, waiting for You,

soul's thirst, heart's ache... that You gave me too.
If He showers grace and help comes from Guru...
I'll let go of my self and unite with the Lord, too!
I will live a life of humility and only think of You:
if we sing Your praises daily we'll be born, anew!
Your Name's the treasure, heart treasures it too,
without it we're a beggar, it's given by the Guru!
O friend, my sacrifice of life to that One is true:
to that One I offer it and all my weaknesses too!
I lose me praising You and I always think of You:
my house is peaceful, since Word gave the Guru;
now I'm always drenched in nectar of bliss, too!
Name is pure, sweet essence taking us to You...
this, gave me sight and union... given by Guru!
Through You, Brahma, Indra are powerful too...
Nanak says: Your Name, I need it to live, I do!

If God gives alms, then the beggar's delighted
and if he eats food the hungry one is delighted.
By meeting the Guru the disciple is delighted:
God... let me see You, let my wish be fulfilled!
Cakvi bird when the sun is in face is delighted:
she gives up suffering then meets her beloved.

Being Guru's favourite… devotee is delighted.

When drinking with mouth baby is delighted:

when it sees its mother, its heart is delighted.

When Guru favours disciple, he is delighted.

In delusion of Illusion all others are delighted:

it is passing away and is a false glass, plated!

Nanak says: one, the real Guru, is delighted!

Yoga isn't in rags dressing, ashes on body, staff carrying:

it is not in shaving of the head or through conch blowing!

He with collyrium of wisdom on eyes Him in all is seeing.

That one is seeing that One, who the One in all is seeing!

Yoga isn't in cemeteries, or in pilgrimage spots wandering;

one does never outside of oneself, it be really discovering.

If with true wisdom you see, God in your eyes is staying.

Stay in your house if the true Teacher you're discovering.

Your illusion will go, Word will be heard, bliss be having

and die while living… and fruit of Yoga be experiencing.

Nanak says: the Word in your heart, always be hearing!

Ah, it's a shame, you slept all night, in day fed the body:

your life a priceless diamond you spent like it was a pea.

Fool, you'll be sorry if His Name you don't take, finally.

On wealth don't depend, at death it goes: with God be!

Don't build hope on your works, His grace is given free!

Your deeds don't fulfil your desires, His will is destiny.

Remember... yours, world's Creator knows, absolutely!

Nanak: all of worth is given to, who He finds worthy.

I've God's Name: from God pain of separation I'm suffering,
my dear!

May I meet my Lord, my Friend, so that comfort I am having,
my dear.

O mother, I have seen the One, the Lord, and I am still living,
my dear.

The Name's my Friend and Teacher, and God me is teaching
my dear.

O pure one, of the qualities of my Lord, my God, be singing...
my dear.

O devotee, be saying His Name, your worth will be growing,
my dear.

The Name of God, the Beloved, the Name of God be saying
my dear.

Through waters of existence you'll no longer be wandering...
my dear.

How will I see God? In my heart and soul is a great longing, my dear.

O pure one, bring Him, in this heart of mine is much loving,

my dear.

By Word of the Guru, God is obtained, the one true King...

my dear.

O you who are the most fortunate, that Name be repeating,

my dear.

In my heart and soul for the Lord, Krishna, is much longing

my dear.

O you holy one, to me, God, the Lord, Krishna... be joining,

my dear.

By instruction of the real Guru, Name keeps on manifesting

my dear.

Nanak says: this way the desire in the heart one is getting,

my dear.

SURDAS (1478-1581) Surdas started praising Lord Krishna since he was young. It is said that he was born in Braj, near Mathura. Surdas was born blind and because of this he was neglected by his family. As a result, he left his home at the age of six.

A chance meeting with the saint Vallabharacharya at Gau Ghat by the river Yamuna in his teens transformed his life. Shri Vallabhacharya taught Surdas lessons in Hindu philosophy and meditation and put him in the path of spirituality. Since Surdas could recite the entire *Srimad Bhagavatam* and was musically inclined, his guru advised him to sing the *'Bhagavad Lila'* – devotional lyrical ballads in praise of Lord Krishna and Radha. Surdas lived in Vrindavan with his guru, who initiated him to his own religious order and later appointed him as the resident singer at Srinath temple in Govardhan.

Surdas' lilting music and fine poetry attracted many laurels. As his fame spread far and wide, the Mughal emperor Akbar (1542-1605) became his patron. He spent the last years of his life in Braj and lived on the donations which he received in return of his *bhajan* singing and lecturing on religious topics, until he died. Surdas also attained fame for his purity of devotion towards Lord Krishna.

Surdas is known for his greatest work ... the *Sur Sagar*. This famous collection is originally said to contain 100,000 songs, however, only 8000 remain today. These songs present a vivid description of the childhood play of Krishna. He also composed *Sur-Saravali,* (that is based on the theory of genesis and the festival of Holi), and *Sahitya-Lahiri,* devotional lyrics dedicated to the Supreme Absolute. Surdas' poetry is also credited as one that lifted the literary value of the Hindi language, transforming it from a crude to a pleasing tongue. Surdas was called the sun in the sky of Hindi literature.

The philosophy of Surdas is a reflection of the times. He was very much immersed in the *Bhakti* movement that was sweeping North India. This movement represented a grass roots spiritual empowerment of the masses. The corresponding spiritual movement of the masses happened in South India in the first millennium. Surdas' poetry was a dialect of Hindi language, Brij Bhasha, until then considered to be a very plebeian language, as the prevalent literary languages were either Persian or Sanskrit. The works of Surdas immediately raised the status of Brij Bhasha from a crude language to that of a literary language of great repute. Due to the training he received from his guru Vallabhacharya, Surdas was a proponent of the Shuddhadvaita school of Vaishnavism (also known as Pushti Marg). This philosophy is based upon the spiritual metaphor of the *Radha-Krishna Rasleela* (The celestial dance between Radha and Lord Krishna). It propagates the path of Grace of God rather than of merging in Him, which seems an extension of the belief of earlier saints like Kabir (see his section previously).

Further Reading...

Rosary of Hymns: Selected Poems of Surdas, Translated by Jaikishandas Sadani, Wiley Eastern Limited, New Delhi, 1991.
Minstrels of God Part 2 by Bankey Behari, Bharatiya Vidya Bhavan, Bombay, 1970. (Pages 207-224).
Divine Sports of Krishna: Poems of Surdas, Translation by A.J. Alston, Shanti Sadan, 1993.
Feel Your Thirst, Poems of Quest, Temple Songs: Surdas. Hrdaipress 1997.
Surdas (Makers of Indian Literature), Usha Nilsson Translator, Sahitya Akademi, New Delhi, 1982.
The Memory of Love: Surdas Sings to Krishna, Translated by John Stratton Hawley, Oxford University Press, 2009.
Three Bhakti Voices: Mirabai, Surdas and Kabir in Their Times and Ours, John Stratton Hawley, Oxford University Press, 2012.
Poems to the Child-God: Structures and Strategies in the Poetry of Surdas by Kenneth E. Bryant, University of California Press, 1979.
Surdas the Blind Saint by O.P. Ralham, Anmol Publications 2005.

Wikipedia article.

Bhajans...

Good or bad, whatever, we belong to You!
Lord, You alone can save me from slander, disgrace too!
Giving up all, to heart I hold Your lotus-feet... O You!
I've lost fear, that I'm bold from Your strength, is true!
I'm aware of this truth... all gods beg at Your door too!
Surdas is happy and secure because of grace from You!

With You I'll live, as You wish I'll be living!
You know heart's pain and desire, why go on repeating?
Kind One, it matters if You give me food... or nothing,
or if one day I ride on an elephant or a load be carrying?
Dark, lotus-eyed Darling, Your slave I'm always being!
You're a boon, blessing to the devotee, Surdas is saying.

Of shame I die, hide, pray You'll forgive me.
From my head down to my feet I am in sin, completely!
I am so disgusting that You will never find one like me.
I passed childhood, manhood and old age, all... sinfully!
My sins none had done, and coming they will never be!

I'm so rotten even hell won't find a corner space for me.
Lord... You should not proud of 'Redeemer of fallen' be,
as You seem to be redeeming those small sinners, only.
Surdas believes Your name if of him redeemer You be!

Lord, a great service to me You're rendering!
You gave me birth to know, but I wasted it by sinning.
Upturned in mother's womb, me You weren't ignoring.
Me from burning hell in stomach You were protecting.
Since my birth I sinned so often, now ruined I'm being.
Of all fallen You are the redeemer... Surdas is stating.

Who should I relate my tale of suffering to?
I'm consumed by mind's agony, heart's burning up too!
In the wild or at home, night or day I'm burnt through!
I often lose hope from worry, think... me drown, I'll do!
Without lotus-eyed Krishna can one live? Surdas too?

What Krishna says will come, will happen!
If one thinks we can change fate, it's a mistake, then!
And so, wash away belief in acts, *mantras,* for when
Krishna decides your fate, none can change it, again!
Why waste time about good or bad, or how or when?

Surdas says, "Let mind on His kind feet lay, again!"

Krishna catches heart in His net of beauty!
See His captivating look, eyebrow curving sensually!
Sandal-paste upon forehead shoots rays, cooling me!
Curls, serpents drinking nectar on forehead, thirsty!
Compared to twin rivers are His two eyebrows, see:
they're like Ganges and Jamuna on face, obviously!
The *gopis* * feel drowned when such beauty, they see!
They can't cross the ocean of Krishna's blue beauty!

*Note: Gopis, young female cowherders, lovers of Krishna.

Radha cries, "I couldn't enjoy Krishna, fully!
Seeing Him these eyes were full of joy, blinding me.
I was upset that due to them I couldn't that One see:
I tried hard to hold them back but they overcame me.
Maybe they saw eyelids as guards, acting forcefully!"
Says Radha, "Why complain of their acts? Tell me!
Krishna is at fault, for revealing His great beauty."

"Gopis, why keep the body without Krishna?
We are obliged to drink poison, for of no use we are!

Either climb to top of mountain and fall down, far...
or, burn self to ashes... or drown self in the Jamuna!
It's so difficult, this painful time, without Krishna!"
Surdas says, "Pining away for Krishna, is Radha."

Gopi! Look at Krishna, truly a sea of beauty!
We cannot cross with these minds such a vast sea!
He's the blue sea, yellow costume waving brightly.
His gait is like a whirlpool, He walks majestically!
Fish-shaped eyes, crocodile-shape earrings, snaky
arms; on breast necklaces like twin Ganges, pearly:
nails, crown like stars, moon, in deep water to see!
Is His form made from Divine Nectar... perfectly?
Gopis seeing His form try to know it, see it closely
but, lose themselves gazing in that sea of Beauty!

No one falling into Love's trap, life enjoyed!
Moth loved the candle, with death was rewarded:
black bee loved the lotus, of life's wealth was bled!
Deer loved hunter's horn, losing life when trapped.
Gopis who loved Krishna now cannot be helped...
Surdas says: "I'm the same, to Him I surrendered."

Gopis say, "Our eyes long for His fine beauty!
Eyelids flutter like fly's wings by fingers held tightly.
Cut from life's nectar, we fruitlessly wait, anxiously!
We *gopis* so tired from searching, sit... unable to flee!
Lonely, like trapped insects we hit heads, repeatedly.
Only if He returns, we will be fish back in the Sea!"

Gopi, without Krishna all turns against Radha!
Her rosy face turns sallow and pale without Krishna!
Her eyes like blooming lotus' now like dry leaves are!
Her gold body now like one burnt by fire does appear.
Her beautiful back's lean, a plantain-trunk no longer!
Surdas: "Her beauty went, separated from Krishna!"

"*Gopi,* where shall I go? I have now lost the way!
I didn't see where He went, I was lost in Him all day!
In the wilds I seek Beloved, this pain in me does stay!
As I tended love's wound He found time to slip away.
In the forest I seek Him, from town and home I stray!
I ask the trees where He went... none shows the way!

I wander seeking Him, crazily... I roam the day away.
If I find Him again, I will not leave Him again, I say.
I'll sit Him in my heart, close my eyes' door that day
and dance with Him, Radha says," Surdas does say!

O Krishna, why this one do You keep forgetting?
You know my inner desires and how I've been acting!
Countless fallen ones You saved... earth inhabiting!
From them You chose me, in shame I'm now sinking!
Born deluded often, finally to You I'm surrendering!
Why at this time be forsaking me? It is frightening!
You redeem sinners, so... why me not be redeeming?
You think Surdas unfit? For Yourself him be saving.

O *gopi*, let us be stealing the flute of that One.
Krishna's enslaved by it, our love still hasn't begun!
Home or out, day or night, always with His lips on.
In His hands, on His lips, or His waist it lies upon.
We don't know its spell, so He knows no other one.
Surdas... "His heart His tunes bind, O that One!"

When in the forest His flute they were hearing,
all *gopis* oblivious of work, home, were wondering...

gave up family ways, *vedic*-codes, were not fearing.

Ocean Krishna, *gopis* streams... in water mingling.

Some prepared, by their bodies with oil anointing.

At night to forest they went as they were, hurrying.

Fearful of sons, husbands, all... they weren't being!

Surdas... "Hearts were captured, by His fluting!"

MIRA BAI (1498-1563). Mira, a Rajput princess was born in Kudki (Kukari), a little village near Merta City that is presently in the Nagaur district of Rajasthan in northwest India. Her father, Ratan Singh, was the youngest son of Rao Duda ruler of Merta and belonged to the Rathore clan. Rao Duda was son of Rao Jodha ruler and founder of Jodhpur.

As a child Mira became deeply enamored by an idol of Girdhar Gopal, Lord Krishna, owned by a holy man; she was inconsolable until she possessed it and kept it all her life. She was highly influenced by her father as he was a worshiper of Krishna.

Mira's mother, Veer Kumari, died during child-birth when Mira was around seven. Mira was then sent to her grandfather, Rao Duda and her father's older brother, Rao Viram Dev at Merta. It is here that she received her education.

Her uncle, Rao Viram Dev arranged Mira's marriage in 1516 when she was eighteen, with prince Bhoj Raj the son of Rana Sanga of Chittor. She was not happy with her marriage as she considered herself already married to Krishna. She went to live in Chittor accompanied by her childhood friend Mithula, who stayed with Mira until the end. Her new family did not approve of her piety and devotion when she refused to worship their family deity, Tulaja Bhawani (Durga).

The Rajputana had remained fiercely independent of the Delhi Sultanate, the Islamic regime that otherwise ruled Hindustan after the conquests of Timur. But in the early 16th century the central Asian conqueror Babur laid claim to the Sultanate and some Rajputs supported him while others ended their lives in battle with him. Her husband's death in battle (in 1521) was only one of a series of losses Mira experienced. Her father-in-law, Rana Sanga respected and protected Mira Bai. However; he also died after a few years and Mira was then persecuted by the rest of her in-laws. She found Krishna to be her only support and rebuked the instructions of her in-laws to give up her worship of Giridhar Gopal. Her grief turned into a passionate spiritual devotion that inspired in her countless poems drenched with separation and longing.

Mira's love to Krishna was at first a private thing but at • some moment it overflowed into an ecstasy that led her to sing and dance in public. She would quietly leave the Chittor fort at night and join *Satsangs* (religious get togethers) in the town below. Her brother-in-law, the new ruler of Chittorgarh, Vikramaditya, was a cruel youth who strongly objected to her devotion, her mixing with commoners and carelessness of feminine modesty. Vikramaditya made several attempts to kill her. Her sister-in-law Uda Bai is also said to have spread defamatory gossip. Raja Vikramaditya tried to harm Mira in many ways such as poisoning and sending her a snake (see *bhajan* following) but she was always saved by Krishna's intervention.

At some time Mira declared herself a disciple of the Spiritual Master Ravidas. After unbearable torture she left • Chittor. First she went to Merta where she was still not satisfied and after sometime left for the centre of Krishnaism, Vrindavan.

She considered herself to be a reborn *gopi*, Lalita, mad with love for Krishna. Folklore informs us of a particular incident where she expressed her desire to engage in a discussion about spiritual matters with Rupa Goswami, a direct disciple of Chaitanya and one of the foremost saints of Vrindavan at that time who, being a renunciated celibate, refused to meet a woman. Mira replied that the only true man in this universe is Lord Krishna.

She continued her pilgrimage, dancing from one village to another, almost covering the whole north of India. She seems to have spent her last years as a pilgrim in Dwarka, Gujarat. It is said that Mira Bai disappeared into the Dwarkadhish Murti

(Image of Lord Krishna) in front of a full audience of onlookers.

Mira's songs or *bhajans* are in a simple form usually composed in simple rhythms with a repeating refrain, collected in her *Padavali*. The extant versions are in a Rajasthani and *Braj*, a dialect of Hindi spoken in and around Vrindavan (the childhood home of Krishna), sometimes mixed with Rajasthani.

She speaks of a personal relationship with Krishna as her lover, Lord and Master. Her poetry is about complete surrender. Her longing for union with Krishna is predominant: she wants to be 'coloured with the colour of dusk' (the colour of Krishna). In Rajasthan, *bhajans* of Mira are still common in religious night gathering known as 'Ratijuga' organized by women.

There have been many movies and plays in India based on her life and countless recordings of her *bhajans*.

Further Reading...

Mira Bai: Her Life and Times by Hermann Goetz, Bharatiya Vidya Bhavan, Bombay. 1966.
The Devotional Poems of Mirabai, Translation with Introduction and Notes by A.J. Alston, Motilal Banarsidas, Delhi, 1980.
Songs of Meera: Lyrics in Ecstasy, Translated by Baldoon Dhingra, Orient Paperbacks, 1977.
Bhakta Mira... by Bankey Behari, Bharatiya Vidya Bhavan, 1971.
Mira Bai and Her Pades, Translation by Krishna P. Bahadur, Munshiram Manoharial, Publishers, New Delhi, 1998.
Mira Bai, by U.S. Nilsson, Sahitya Akademi, New Delhi, 1969.
Minstrels of God, Part One, by Bankey Behari, Bharatiya Vidya Bhavan, Bombay. 1956 (Pages 66-118).
Mystic Songs of Meera, Translated by V.K. Subramanian, Abhinav Publications, New Delhi, 2005.
Meera Bai by B.K. Chaturvedi, Low Price Publications, New Delhi, 2002.
Meera Bai and Her Poetry by Giriraj Sharan Agarwal, Diamond Pocket Books, 2010.
In the Dark of the Heart, Songs of Meera: A New Translation of the Much-Loved Songs of the Sixteenth-Century Poet-Saint of India. Translated by Shamsa Futehally, Harper Collins, San Francisco, 1998.
Wikipedia Article.

Bhajans...

You, are my companion in life and in death too...
in this life I'm living I'll never be forsaking You!
I, cannot be comforted unless I am seeing You...
be asking my heart it will be witness to this too!
To seek a glimpse of You I go climbing higher to
see and nightly I'm weeping: I can't get through.
This world is an illusion, it is false, it is untrue...
all relationships are false, connections false too.
I stand here with my hands folded, begging You:
listen to my prayer, Your ear lend me, please do!
My mind raced like a mad elephant's... it's true:
until my Master calmed it, it raged on through!
Now, that always His presence I have is true...
at Girdhar Gopal's* feet is always Mira... too!

*Note: Girdhar Gopal is Mira's personal name for Lord Krishna.

O Darling, for You all comforts I was forsaking...
why is it, that now away from me You're staying?

With the fire of separation this heart is burning...
O please come to me now... and me be comforting!
As it is not possible for me to be from it escaping,
can You please come smiling, and me be meeting.
Through many lifetimes Mira to You is belonging
so why do not You come and her... be embracing?

O my Dear, the vision of You be giving to me...
this separation I can't take, it goes on endlessly.
Like waterless lotus and moonless night, I'll be
suffering without Your presence, endless agony!
Longing, I rush everywhere, no resting for me...
while separation from You eats me up inwardly.
This, my tale of suffering I can't tell, as nightly
I go on without sleep, days with no food for me.
Only You can listen to and understand and see
this tale I can't truly tell, so come and help me!
With pain of separation why torture me cruelly?
Come to me, You who live in my heart already.
Mira is still Your slave... she kneels obediently
before You, begging; own her, let her Yours be!

O Krishna, complaint of Your slave be hearing...

to me who is totally devoted to You be listening.
I've become mad because to see You I'm longing;
separation's vicious circle, me has been crushing.
Really, for Your sake a *yogin* * I'll be becoming,
and in the wilderness I'll wander... You seeking.
Upon my body white ashes I shall be sprinkling
and with skin of a deer my body I'll be wrapping.
O Eternal One, again today we're not meeting,
as through the wilderness I wander... weeping!
Mira, suddenly her Lord Girdhar was seeing...
He consoled her and over was all her suffering.
Each fibre of her body peace was then finding...
lifetimes ended as He her was forever claiming.

*Note: Yogin... a female Yogi.

Now that You've made me a consort, save me...
Lord, my hand in Yours be taking, permanently!
You are omnipotent, I surrender to You totally;
O You, Who all actions bring about eventually.
Currents of ocean of change are terrible to see...
please, You... ship to take me across, be for me!
You, world's Teacher, shelter of shelterless, see

how You are the refuge of all, so be that for me!
Through the ages You've helped every devotee
from cycles of rebirth... saving them eternally.
And so, it is right that You save from calumny
and gossip Mira, lying at Your feet obediently.

Lord, please give a compassionate look my way!
Before You Mira stands in prayer, here, today...
but, I do not see You my kind Lord, in any way!
All my kin are now foes and treat me hard, I say.
My captain and saviour is only You... so I pray
to You as my boat in rough waters works away.
I am standing here in great pain, hurting today,
knowing no sleep at night... or peace in the day.
Separation's arrow put my heart in a bad way:
not for one moment can I forget its pain, I say.
Lord, although Ahalya* was of stone, by way
of one touch You saved her... come what may!
You find in light Mira, much weight... today?
Why do You hesitate to save her? Please say!

*Note: Ahalya, the wife of Gautama Maharishi was cursed to become a
stone and regained her human form after she was brushed by Lord Rama's
foot.

Let me now the praises of Govinda be singing:
if the Raja's upset, his kingdom I'll be leaving.
If the Lord should be with me angry, nothing
can I do, to what kingdom will I be traveling?
When the Raja sent me poison to be drinking
I found it to be nectar, all... I was swallowing.
And when the Raja a black cobra was sending
a garland in its place... I was then discovering.
In ecstasy of joy, now Mira is herself finding;
for, her consort in her Lord, she is now seeing!

Without the Lord Krishna, my house is empty:
who can take me to the Beloved... to Him see?
To be taken to Him I'd give my soul and body:
because of Him I wander in forest, aimlessly!
I dress up in an ochre robe so He can see me!
Hour that we were to meet has gone, clearly

You have not yet come to meet me, I can see.
Look at my hair, it's become grey, suddenly!
Mira's Lord, when do You come to meet me

now that I've given up all for You... totally?

For only a moment I lay down upon my bed,
my eyes I closed... I wondered, I pondered.
Suddenly... it was my Lord Who appeared
glancing so fast; I rose His feet I touched.
Then I woke up as if I had been startled...
in a moment Beloved had left I discovered.
By sleeping many others Him have missed:
though I woke up, Him gone I discovered!
It is Girdhar Gopal that is Mira's Lord...
all are happy, for gone home has the Lord!

Without Krishna, from longing I am not sleeping:
the flame of love drives me to be to be wandering.
Without Beloved my house is dark, no lighting...
any lamp that I light to me is no longer pleasing.
And, without my Beloved my bed is uninviting...
and so all of the nights wide awake I am passing.
When will my Beloved to my home be returning?
The frogs are croaking the peacocks are crying...
and I listen, the cuckoo's song I am now hearing.
Now... I see the low, black clouds are gathering!

Lightning's flashing, fear in the heart it's stirring.

Eyes full of tears: what to do, where to be going?

This pain I am suffering, who can it be stopping?

The snake of absence, this body has been biting.

And now this life that I have left away is ebbing

with each beat of my heart now slowly stopping.

Quickly bring that herb that me will be saving!

Which friend will the Beloved to me be bringing?

Lord, when will You come, to Mira be meeting?

O my Heartcharmer, with delight me be filling!

Lord, when will You come to with me be talking?

TULSIDAS (1532-1623). Tulsidas (also known as Goswami Tulsidas) was a Hindu poet-saint, reformer and philosopher renowned for his devotion for the Avatar, Rama. A composer of several popular works, he is best known for being the author of the epic *Ramcharitmanas,* a retelling of the Sanskrit *Ramayana* in the vernacular Awadhi. Tulsidas was acclaimed in his lifetime to be a reincarnation of Valmiki, the composer of the original *Ramayana* in Sanskrit. He is also considered to be the composer of the *Hanuman Chalisa,* a popular devotional hymn dedicated to Hanuman, the divine monkey helper and devotee of Rama.

Tulsidas lived permanently and died in the city of Varanasi. The Tulsi Ghat in Varnasi is named after him. He founded the Sankatmochan Temple dedicated to Hanuman in Varanasi, believed to stand at the place where he had the sight of Hanuman.

Tulsidas started the Ramlila plays, a folk-theatre adaption of the *Ramayana.* He has been acclaimed as one of the greatest poets in Hindi, Indian, and world literature. The impact of Tulsidas and his works on the art, culture and society in India is widespread and is seen to date in vernacular language,

Ramlila plays, Hindustani classical music, popular music, and television series.

His parents were Hulsi and Atmaram Dubey. Most sources identify him as a Saryupareen Brahmin of the Parashar Gotra (lineage), although some sources claim he was a Kanyakubja or Sanadhya Brahmin.

According to the *Mula Gosain Charita* and some other works, Tulsidas was married to Ratnavali who was the daughter of Dinbandhu Pathak, a Brahmin of the Bharadwaja Gotra, who belonged to Mahewa village of Kaushambi district. They had a son named Tarak who died as a toddler. Once when Tulsidas had gone to a Hanuman temple, Ratnavali went to her father's home with her brother. When Tulsidas came to know this, he swam across the Yamuna river in the night to meet his wife. Ratnavali chided Tulsidas for this, and remarked that if Tulsidas was even half as devoted to God as he was to her body of flesh and blood, he would have been redeemed. Tulsidas left her instantly and left for the holy city of Prayag. Here, he renounced the Grihastha (householder's life) stage and became a Sadhu (Hindu ascetic).

He started composing poetry in Sanskrit in Varanasi on the Prahlada Ghat. Tradition holds that all the verses that he composed during the day, would get lost in the night. This happened daily for eight days. On the eighth night, Shiva – whose famous Kashi Vishwanath Temple is located in Varanasi – is believed to have ordered Tulsidas in a dream to compose poetry in the vernacular instead of Sanskrit. Tulsidas woke up and saw both Shiva and Parvati who blessed him. Shiva ordered Tulsidas to go to Ayodhya and compose poetry in Awadhi. Shiva also predicted that Tulsidas' poetry would fructify like the *Sama Veda*. In the *Ramcharitmanas,* Tulsidas hints at having the Darshan of Shiva and Parvati in both dream and awakened state.

In the year 1575 Tulsidas started composing the *Ramcharitmanas* in Ayodhya. He composed the epic over two years, seven months and twenty-six days. It is mainly in *slokas,* with occasional *dohas.*

Towards the end of his life he suffered from very painful boils that affected his arms. At this time he wrote the *Hanuman Bahuk,* which begins with a verse in praise of Hanuman's strength, glory, and virtue, and is followed by a prayer to relieve him of his unbearable arm pain. The disease was cured.

Major Works: *Ramacharitamanas*... literally 'The Holy Lake of Acts of Rama', is the Awadhi rendering of the *Ramayana* narrative. Dohavali (1581), literally 'Collection of

Dohas', is a work consisting of 573 miscellaneous *Doha* and *Sortha* verses mainly in Braja with some verses in Awadhi (see following). *Kavitavali* (1608–1614), literally 'Collection of Kavittas', is a Braja rendering of the *Ramayana,* composed entirely in metres of the Kavitta family – Kavitta, Savaiya, Ghanakshari and Chhappaya. *Gitavali,* literally 'Collection of Songs', is a Braja rendering of the *Ramayana* in songs. *Krishnavali* (1607), literally 'Collection of Songs to Krishna', is a collection of 61 songs in honor of Krishna in Braja. *Vinaya Patrika,* literally 'Petition of Humility', is a Braja work consisting of 279 stanzas or hymns.

Further Reading...

The Ramayana of Tulasidasa, Translated from the Original by F.S. Growse, Motilal Banarsidass, Delhi, Revised edition 1978.

The Holy Lake of the Acts of Rama: A New English Translation of Tulasi Das's Ramacaritanansa by W. Douglas P. Hill, Oxford University Press London, 1952.

Sri Ramacaritamanasa or (The Manasa lake brimming over with the exploits of Sri Ramao with Hindi Text and English Translation, Gita Press, Gorakhpur. (date?)

Kavitavali: Tulsi Das, Translated and with a Critical Introduction by F.R. Allchin, George Allen & Unwin Ltd, London, 1964.

Selected Dohas, Translated into English by K.C. Kanda, Lotus Press, New Delhi, 2008. (Pages 56-85).

Hanuman Chalisa of Tulsidasi: (With English Translation and Notes) Khemraj Shrikrishnadass, 1996.

Complete Works of Goswami Tulsidas: Translated by S.P. Bahadur, Munshiram Manoharlal Publishers, New Delhi, 1996.

The Philosophy of Tulsidas by Ramdat Bharadwaj, Munshiram Manoharlal Publishers, New Delhi, 1979.

Tulsidas by Shiv & S. Ram Gajrani, Commonwealth Publishers, 2011.

Wikipedia article.

Dohas...

Family... sons and daughters, can turn one evil:
to listen to spiritual talks makes one more civil.

See another's wife as your mother or another's
gold:
Tulsidas is advising that this is how to love
Gold!

From greed anger is coming; death is from anger, no less...
religion's soul is compassion, God's breath is forgiveness.

Where you are unwelcome and receive no respect
there,
from place like that stay away, even if riches are
there.

Virtue's soul is compassion and evil seed is vanity;
as long as you breathe cling to compassion, tightly.

Selfishness is what is driving one's love and hate;
one wealthy with property, friends will highly rate.

To those who are wealthy wealth runs... with arms
open;
but, Tulsi, all of those who are poor sleep out in the
open.

Do not relate to a filthy mind, it might rub off on you...
if you toss a stone in a puddle, dirty water on your shoe!

O Tulsi, two things to do if in this world you live:
meditate upon Rama and food to the hungry give.

Stay true in actions and words, don't brag about success:
if you do wrong, just repenting won't clean up the mess!

If you wish a friend to be testing, there are three ways:
when in trouble or need ask, or live next door for days.

If wealthy beyond belief... and this world ruling
you are,
power and wealth is useless if of death thinking
you are!

If in your heart lust, rage, pride or greed keeps staying,
even if you are intelligent, wisdom you are not having.

Be loving to all you meet and treat them warmly:
one doesn't know how God may manifesting be!

One who looks finds, and God inside is residing:
in temples or far off, this stupid world is seeking.

Look for knowledge everywhere, from low or high,
look even in the dirt because Gold in there can lie.

If you act before you think, you'll get into trouble:
"Look before you leap," is said; remember it well!

A two-legged thing is wealth, from front and behind
kicking...
making us lose our head coming and a broken mind...
going!

Take this advice I offer you: all necessities store up!
When needed, even price of clay will one day go up!

God's sacred name keep saying, yourself in God be losing:
all the wrong thoughts in you will immediately be leaving.

If you sow seed of the acacia can you get a mango?
The truth is well-known: you reap, what you sow!

At root tongue might wither, away waste the body,
as each day passes stronger is faith of the devotee.

Even in good company all who are mean, mean stay...
if snake lies in a sandalwood tree it still strikes away!

Rama is the number one, all else naught, nothing:
the one can become many, nothing stays nothing!

O Tulsi, in this world these actions are the most gainful:
meditation, selfless service, going to gatherings spiritual.

Don't be leaving your home or upset your family:
have faith in Rama's grace, do life's tasks, daily.

To Rama yourself be pledging, at His feet surrendering,
His grace will be blessing you and real peace be giving.

Lasting joy and real peace sweet words will bring you:
give up harsh words if you want the world to love you.

All think only of self, a few for others are feeling…
the few are liked and loved, who others are helping.

In rags they wrap themselves, walk with skulls in hand,
as holy men they are faking in this iron age, in this land.

Body is the field and mind the one who is ploughing…
seeds are good and evil, what you sow you are reaping.

Scholars, saints and soldiers, all those of good actions,
if greed spoils them their magic leaves all their actions.

On God concentrate and close your mouth, ears, eyes:
if outside doors are shut, inner window is open to eyes.

Slokas from his Ramayana

I bow to the feet of Valmiki who created the Ramayana...
though telling about the demon Khara, cousin of Ravana
is soft, charming, faultless too; often of Dusana* talking.
And I praise all the four Vedas* too, like barques sailing
on the ocean of illusory existence... that are never tired
of singing of Shri Rama's glory: He is the Ragus' head!
I welcome that dust upon Brahma's* feet... the evolver
worldly existence's ocean which is birthplace of nectar:
cow and the moon so plentiful as in saints' appearing...
and poison and wine in the form of the evil, appearing!
Bowing to feet of gods, Brahmans, wise presiding over

nine planets, with joined palms I pray: help my desire!

*Notes: Dusana was another cousin like Khara of the demon-king of Sri Lanka, Ravana. The Vedas are a large body of texts originating in ancient India. Composed in Vedic Sanskrit, the texts constitute the oldest layer of Sanskrit literature and the oldest scriptures of Hinduism. Brahma is God the Creator.

Slokas from Kavitavali

At dawn to Lord of Avadh's door I was going

when with a child in his arms came the king…

I stood stunned on seeing that dispeller of woe,

and who aren't like me stunned, gather a blow.

Tulsi says: mind was pleased by the boy's eyes

with collyrium adorned, like a wagtail, restless;

my dear, like two, fresh, blue lotuses it seemed,

of equal beauty, upon the moon there bloomed!

Anklets on feet, on each lotus-hand, a bracelet…

and a bright jewel-garland on His lovely breast:

on his fresh, dark form, a yellow shirt shining…

the king, on his lap taking Him, was laughing!

EKNATH (1533-1599). He was a prominent Marathi saint, scholar and religious poet. In the development of Marathi literature, Eknath is seen as a bridge between the towering predecessors Dnyaneshwar and Namdev and his equally noble successors Tukaram and Ramdas. Eknath was born in an illustrious Brahmin family of Pratisthan (Paithan today). They were said to be the Kulkarnis of the village, his real name is Eknath Suryajipant Kulkarni. Saint Bhanudas who brought back the sacred image of Lord Pandurang from Vijaynagar to Pandharpur was Eknath's great grandfather.

Eknath was born under the star sign of 'Mula' in the Sagittarius constellation, traditionally considered a bad omen for the parents of the child. The omen was borne out for Eknath's father Suryanarayan and mother Rukmini who died shortly after his birth and Eknath was brought up by his grandparents, Chakrapani and Saraswatibai. As an orphan, Eknath had to suffer the taunts of other children. He began avoiding their company and found refuge as a child in prayer and other devotional practices.

When about twelve Eknath heard about Janardana. This great scholar and Guru lived in Devgiri renamed as

Daulatabad by the Muslim rulers of the time. Eager to become his disciple, Eknath trudged all the way to Devgiri. Janardana was amazed by this extraordinarily gifted boy and readily accepted him as his disciple. He taught Eknath Vedanta, Nyaya, Meemansa, Yoga etc. and most importantly, Saint Dnyaneshwar's works. Janardana was a devotee of Lord Dattatreya (Govinda or Krishna) and this meant that Eknath's social and religious outlook consisted of tolerance and kindness toward all fellow beings. Many of Eknath's poems are in praise of his master.

He asked Eknath to go on a pilgrimage. He himself accompanied Eknath up to Nasik-Tryambakeshwar. There, Eknath wrote his famous treatise on the *Chatushloki Bhagavat*. In this Marathi commentary, he explained the significance of four sacred *slokas* of the *Bhagavat* in 1036 specially metered verses known as *ovee*.

After completing his pilgrimage, consisting of various holy places of west and north India, Eknath returned to Paithan. His grandparents were extremely delighted to see him again and implored him to marry. His wife Girija and he were truly made for each other and established an ideal examples of ethical living. In time, the couple was blessed with two daughters, Godavari and Ganga and a son Hari.

Eknath was responsible for the rediscovery of the great work of Dnyaneshwar (see his section previously), the first great poet of Marathi literature, the epic poem the *Dnyaneshwari*, his commentary on the *Bhagavad Gita* which had been forgotten like many after the Muslim invasions. During the intervening period between Dnyaneshwar and Eknath, Maharashtra, like the rest of the country, had been ravaged by Muslim invasions. Eknath saw that the need of the hour was a revival of Marathi literature, of the great epics, an education in the old values and if the once popular Marathi-worded *Dnyaneshwari* could be brought again to the people, they could be uplifted, morally and spiritually. He then devoted a few, hard years in compiling an undistorted version of the *Dnyaneshwari*.

Almost all of Eknath's writings were in verse form in Marathi. Eknath wrote a scholarly and lucid commentary, *Eknathi Bhagavata*, on the Eleventh Canto of the Sanskrit sacred text, the *Bhagavata Purana*. The commentary involved 18,800 couplets. He composed many other books. He introduced a new form of Marathi religious song called *Bharood*, writing 300 of them. He also wrote 4000 religious songs in the *Abhang* form. He was also a preacher, and gave many public discourses.

Eknath initiated in Maharashtra a movement called *Wasudewa Sanstha*. It involved house-to-house visitations by individuals known as *Wasudewa*, who, standing in front of peoples' houses, spread religious messages through *bhajans* (ballads).

Eknath was one of the earliest reformers of untouchability in Maharashtra. In times when Brahmins even avoided the shadow and the voice of an untouchable, he publicly showed courtesy toward untouchables and frequented them. Once he saved the life of a Mahar child, rescuing it from the scorching heat, the child was wandering in the hot sand of the Godavari. The Brahmins of the village got angry at Eknath imparting his touch to the body of an 'untouchable'. In an act meant to mollify them, he famously took a bath in the same river to wash away the *impurity*, hoping they would see the inhumanity of their taboos.

Certain religious poets had dealt with the question of their own death by resorting to a 'samadhi'. Here the poet took his own life by immersing himself in a body of water, such as a lake or a river. Following the example of his idol, Dnyaneshwar, Eknath embraced 'jalsamadhi' (water samadhi) in the sacred Godavari River.

Further Reading...

The Life of Eknath: Sri Eknath Charita by Justin E. Abbott, Motilal Banarsidass, New Delhi, 1981.

Eknath: A Maratha Bhakta by Wilbur Stone Deming, Karnatak Press, Bombay, 1931.

Eknath by G. V. Tagare, Sahitya Akademi, New Delhi, 1993.

Mysticism in Maharashtra by R.D. Ranade, Motilal Banarsidass, Delhi, 1933.

Saints of Maharashtra by Savitribai Khanolkar, Bharatiya Vidya Bhavan, Bombay, 1990. (Pages 103-37).

The Great Integrators: The Saint-Singers of India by Dr. V. Raghavan, Publications Division, New Delhi 1974. (Pp 135-6).

Wikipedia Article.

Abhangs...

Allow my thought always to be upon Govinda!
Ah my mind, let your goal always be Govinda!
O you, most Perfect One, the name of Brahma,
allow my thoughts to be always on... Govinda!
All of the temptations will fall away together...
and, half of the problems will be solved forever!
Govinda is every where, every one is Govinda!
This, says the one who is serving Janardana!

Lord, there is only one request I make of You...
to serve all the Saints by day and by night too.
Let me live at Pandahari, make it come true...
and allow me sing always, my praises of You!
And may Your name always be on my lips too:
this is everything that I am wanting from You.
Janardana says: "Seeing oneself as a true
servant of God is all wishes coming true!
To be such, all wishes are fulfilled... too!"

Guru, the teacher, is the Mother…
and Guru the teacher is the Father,
Guru is clan's God, the Master…
in hard times Guru is my protector!
At Guru's feet I am the surrenderer
of my actions, words, all I can offer.
Janardana, Krishna, my saviour:
to that One alone do I surrender.

Many people, the word 'death' are fearing…
they don't that know one day us it is taking.
The flower dries up and the fruit is coming…
and later on that same fruit is disappearing.
One goes before, another behind is coming:
everything, into hands of death is passing.
All who from name of 'death' are running,
one day on the funeral pile they're placing.
Carriers who dead as heavy are regarding,
one day to a cemetery others are carrying.
"Only who to God are submitting
death leaves"… Eknath is saying.

The Lord of the three worlds is Janardana,
and an account with me opened Janardana.
And... account that was opened was for a
large amount, always in name of... Rama!
As his bond he gave me, "I am Brahma"...
I accepted it reverently for 'He' is no other.
Of garments of love to me he was the giver:
of the leaves of salvation I was the receiver.
I then built city of 'Absorbed into Brahma':
then I went, I sat in fortress of Chaitanya. *
The revenue of Self-knowledge I will gather
and I will send it to Janardana, my Master.
Balance of debt the Saints' will be bringer,
and *Bhakti* will be... that beautiful receiver.
Merit from a previous birth I was acquirer,
such were business relations I had to foster.
I am absolutely satisfied in Janardana!

*Note: Chaitanya Mahaprabhu was a social reformer in eastern India in the 16th century, worshipped by followers of Gaudiya Vaishnavism as the full incarnation of Lord Krishna.

Knowledge, was born from the womb of *Bhakti:*
and the glory of knowledge… is through *Bhakti!*
Knowledge has gained its glory through *Bhakti:*
the root of knowledge and detachment is *Bhakti!*
One, is taken by the darkness without *Bhakti…*
how can there be fruit… without root of *Bhakti?*
One… who does deeds that are tied to *Bhakti*
for Janardana, at feet is knowledge of *Bhakti!*

Death, it came to me, to me be stinging;
but, into merciful Lord it was changing.
Now, that One so well I am knowing…
because heart, that Heart was meeting!
Though all thought of body was going;
death, all of its power was then losing!
Eknath, Janardana on feet is dancing
to tune: life, death has no flavouring.

DADU (1544-1603). Dadu Dayal was a poet/saint from Gujarat, India. "Dadu" means brother, and "Dayal" means "the compassionate one".

He was reputedly found by an affluent business man floating on the river Sabarmati. He later moved to Amer (city), near Jaipur Rajasthan, where he gathered around himself a group of followers, forming a sect that became known as the *Dadu-panth*.

This organization has continued in Rajasthan to the present-day and has been a major source of early manuscripts containing songs by Dadu and other North Indian saints. Dadu's compositions were recorded by his disciple Rajjab and are known as the *Dadu Anubhav Vani*, a compilation of 5,000 couplets. Another disciple, Janagopal, wrote the earliest biography of Dadu.

Dadu alludes to spontaneous (*sahaja*) bliss in his songs. Much of the imagery used is similar to that used by Kabir, and to that used by earlier *Sahajiya* Buddhists and Nath yogis. Dadu believed that devotion to God should transcend religious or sectarian affiliation, and that devotees should become non-sectarian or *nipakh*.

Dadu had 100 disciples that attained *samadhi*. He instructed additional 52 disciples to set up *ashrams* around the region to spread the Lord's word. Dadu spent the latter years of his life in Naraiana, a small distance away from the town of Dudu, near Jaipur city. Five *ashrams* are considered sacred by the followers; Naraiana, Bhairanaji, Sambhar, Amer, and Karadala (Kalyanpura). Followers at these *ashrams* later set up other places of worship.

Further Reading...

A Sixteenth-Century Indian Mystic: Dadu and His Followers by W. G. Orr, Lutterworth Press, London, 1947.
The Hindu Biography of Dadu Dayal by Winard M. Callewaert, Motilal Banarsidass, Delhi, 1988.
Dadu: The Compassionate Mystic, Translated by K.N. Upadhyaya, Radha Soami Satsang Beas, 1979.
Saint Dadu Dayal: Saints of India, by Dr. Sangh Mittra, Criterion Publications, 2002.
Dadu (1544-1604) Translated by Andrew Schelling, Longhouse Publications, Vermont, 2009.
Wikipedia Article.

Bhajans…

O Keshava,* leave me never:

because, You are my Saviour!

Do not throw me away if You see I am a sinner…

Lord be merciful, though sinful is this worshipper!

From birth sinning… head to foot the wrong-doer:

remove all my mistakes; You, the Great Creator!

I am so filthy, make me whole, O Great Forgiver!

My Lord is powerful, O You become my Saviour:

don't forget me, even if I forget You, O Keshava!

To You lead Dadu, do not leave now, this sinner!

*Note: Lord Krishna.

All is for You, eternal companion, O Rama,

wearing ascetic's garb, with ashes myself smear…

that I look for You as a travelling seeker, O Rama:

upon the mountains I stay, on Meru's peak appear,

that I keep calling out to You, calling: "O Rama!"

that I burn up this body, my heart make disappear,

that my head the saw I'm placing under, O Rama:

194

that me I am beheading; it, to You I am the giver:
Dadu... self as sacrifice makes an offer, O Rama!

Lord, what way to You be worshipping, is good?
I don't know way You to be pleasing... is good!
To sing, dance or world's favour be seeking, is good?
To shave head, at sacred places be bathing, is good?
To leave home and family, to be wandering, is good?
To smear body with ashes, hair be growing, is good?
To roam forests and silence be observing... is good?
To do austerities, take on any wise saying, is good?
To say one knows Brahma, be meditating, is good?
Dadu doesn't know, You what, be telling, is good!

Beyond knowing is power of the Almighty,
where is He from and where hiding is He?
The air and the water how did He create? Tell me!
Beyond knowing is the earth and heavens mystery.
How was He planting one's soul inside the body?
How were five elements, to make a home uniting?
How is it possible, for one, to many be appearing?
How is it possible for all, into one, be dissolving?
How does that One... the universe be upholding?

From that power of that One, Dadu's staggering!

How, shall I my Lord Rama ever discover?
The passions I have are beyond me, forever!
In every direction is breaking out my mind, a rover!
It cannot see that Rama is near, but... even closer!
For what is the Truth the ears are not the hearer...
beauty of the form the eyes an enchanter discover!
There is no ending to one's lust and to our anger...
because of greed the heart of things is a possessor!
Dadu says: how is it possible the Lord to discover,
as long as the mind of sensual objects is a desirer?

Ah Rama, Your hand, out be stretching...
You make all happen, here I'm entangling.
I am blind in a deep pit, me... don't be delivering:
only You are mine, Lord of Mercy, all humbling!
Snare of illusion's everywhere, no way appearing:
noose death's drawn tight, who me is delivering?
No Rama, so no escape! O You, me be helping!
A thousand tries, nothing! I'm now in, sinking!
Rama when humble in distress You're seeing...
aren't You all pain and all anguish destroying?

Dadu says: stretch hand, all, You are making!

O heart, love Rama Who gave soul and a body:
Who created heavens, constellations we see...
Who put as lamps the sun and moon, to move freely,
one hot and one cool as they are revolving endlessly;
Who made seven oceans and earth O so colourfully:
Who created water, air and rain falling plentifully...
Who waters countless trees, herbs in great variety!
From five elements He made it all, looking closely.
Love Rama Who woke Dadu from sleep, suddenly!

Let nothing to come between us, Madhava, *
even if You take life, all from me, Madhava!
If You give me pain, misery, comfort, riches, Madhava,
if prince, beggar, in home, forest, sea, shore, Madhava;
if You free me or chain me, give three worlds Madhava,
if You take all penalties, or give deliverance, Madhava;
if You give me a place on earth or in heaven, Madhava,
even if You give to me the sun or the moon, Madhava;
always allow me to be forever close to You, Madhava,
do not ever be far away from Your Dadu... Madhava!

*Note: Lord Krishna.

None thinks of robbing one not sleeping...
waking one is on guard, no thief is coming!
The master of the house if sleeping knows nothing:
thief around his house to take his goods is creeping.
There is not a one, who for that thief is watching...
and so, that thief finds it easy to do all his thieving.
Once the deed is done, what is the use of watching?
Those goods are gone, that night won't be returning!
No harm comes to one's goods if one is not sleeping.
Dadu says: now you know make sure to be watching!

Foolish one, you will not be in this body again:
why are you squandering it... again and again?
When the opportunity's gone you nothing gain;
where... O where shall you be finding it again?
Your good fortune is so great, to this present life attain
in this body so why try to attain such imaginings, vain?
In worldly troubles you have drowned it, trying to obtain
illusion you've mixed the gold with clay... to what gain?
Do not now start thinking that you will find it... again:
don't throw away this opportunity again, use your brain!

That wealth of all of the three worlds is yours, to gain...
if you make the right trade you could be in a higher plane.
As breath is still in your body... why not it try to attain?
Dadu says: he who has body, must take the Lord's name!

Listen, there is no other father but You:
Your names are many, I know only You.
You're the One Indivisible God, merciful Rama is You!
You are the Ruler, Mohan* the Enchanter is You... too!
You are Keshava the Beautiful, Compassionate... True!
You are the Lord, the Creator, the Pure, the Holy too...
You're Changeless, the Disposer, Hari, the Self is You!
You're the Provider, Omnipresent, Many-coloured, too;
the Highest, the Almighty, the King, the Master's You.
Allah... the Imperishable, Bounteous, our Lord is You...
Wonderful, Incomparable! Dadu says: all Names... too!

You're the One who disguises is changing:
though hiding You, don't me be deceiving!
Why be telling me off: are You Yourself now hiding?
How can I live by myself like a woman in mourning?
O my Saviour of my soul, don't me alone be leaving:
always stay with Dadu, him... safely over be taking!

RASAKHAN (1548-1628) was a poet who was both a Muslim and follower of Lord Krishna. His real name was Sayyad Ibrahim and is known to have lived in Amroha in India. In his early years, he became a follower of Lord Krishna and learned from his Spiritual Master Goswami Vitthalnath and began living in Vrindavan and spent his whole life there.

There are differences in the opinion of scholars regarding his year of birth. Rasakhan was the son of a Jagirdar. His family was wealthy, and he received a good education. Raskhan spoke both Hindi (Braj Bhasha or early Urdu) & Persian; he translated 'Bhagavata Purana' into Persian.

His shrine is located in Gokul near the Yamuna river, Bhramand Ghat. It is a very peaceful place. Many Krishna devotees come there to pay their respects & meditate.

The poetry of Rasakhan focuses on Lord Krishna. *Rasakhan Rachnavali* is the collection of Rasakhan's poetry. His creations describe the beauty of not only Lord Krishna but also his relations with his beloved Radha.

Further Reading...

The Poems of Rasakhan: Treasure House of Love by Krishna Kinkari, David Haberman & Shyam Das, Pratham Peeth Publications, 2007.
Indian Mystic Verse Translated by Hari Prasad Shastri, Shanti Sadan, London, 1941 (Pages 134-6).
The Hindu Classical Tradition: A Braj Bhasha Reader by Rupert Snell, School of Oriental & African Studies, University of London, 1991 (Pages 110-122).
Wikipedia Article.

Bhajans...

Be me born again in Braj with cowherders of Gokul as

Rasakhan...

if as a beast I'd graze forever with Nanda's cows, if I

can...

if stone, of His umbrella against Indra's waves, that

mountain...

if a bird, let me nest in tree, where the Yamuna river

ran. *

*Notes: Gokul is the village in Uttar Pradash where Krishna spent his childhood. Nanda... the head of the gopis, female cowherders. Krishna held the mountain Govardhan over to stop the flooding rains sent by the goddess Indra. The Yamuna river is the largest tributary of the Ganges where on its banks Krishna would play will the gopis.

On head I'll put His peacock feather, around neck His seed

necklace...

wrap His yellow sash around, take His stick, walk to *gopis*

place!

He is my Beloved and Rasakhan will imitate Him... to His

face!

But, flute-player's flute He held to his lips, on mine I'll not
place.

For this stick and blanket's sake I'd give up three worlds
sovereignty...
joys of eight talents, nine riches to Nanda's cows graze,
happily.
Rasakhan, when shall I the forests, pools, gardens of Braj
see?
If you made a million palaces I'd give up all for its groves,
thorny!

For Him with *gopis*, with cows, singing, glancing, O eyes
yearn...
garlands of pearls I'd give up for His of seeds, O soul does
burn!
Those mudbrick walls I treasure... to golden palaces I will
turn?
Dvarka's houses are tall, but to Braj's cow-pens heart will
return.

Rasakhan said, "What to tell, to that place you were not

going...

in Braj, all the girls offer their souls to that One they are

blessing!

Thoughts of others none think of, Yadav lord* magic is

performing...

He sang tune, His love cast, our souls delighting, cattle

grazing.

*Note: Lord of the Yadav or caste of cowherders.

Playing flute, singing His song, with *gopis* and cows He

arrived...

with His flute calling all cowherding boys, my name He

sounded.

Fearing mother-in-law, sister-in-law close... my breath I

stopped:

O Rasakhan, how to act? I'm distraught, heart has been

robbed!

Yesterday, Braj's cowherder with *gopis* a Holi dance did do…

He sang a rakish tune delighting hearts, all in the village too.

Squirting, He drenched girls with love, my body danced to

His dancing eyes, mother, sister-in law, rivals too: I shy grew!

Under the spell of His flute Kanha* fell, who now us is loving?

She follows Him day and night… wives in anguish are crying.

Rasakhan, we burn due to who charmer of hearts was charming:

O friend, let us run away… for now the flute in Braj is residing.

*Note: Kanha means a lover of Lord Krishna.

Today a herder's wife went mad, she lost control of her

body...

her mother prayed, mother-in-law asked exorcist her to

see.

Rasakhan called upon all in Braj, but... no one had any

remedy:

none will take from Kanha that small flute, to burn it...

immediately.

I looked for Him in the *Puranas'* songs, in *Vedic* hymns

seeking...

I never saw or heard how His form was, or... His way of

being.

I called, I sought but didn't find, none to Rasakhan was

showing...

but then I saw Him hiding in grove's hut, Radha's feet

massaging.

Ever since I saw Nanda's boy, I cut off all of my ties to

family:

the social graces, what world says... means nothing to

me!

By the beauty of Shyama* my heart is ravished, drunk

blissfully!

As rivers race toss aside all flotsam on the way to the

sea,

my mind now free flows to ocean's infinity. Rasakhan:

"We

each night and day are drinking the honey of Shyama's

beauty!"

*Note: Shyama is the gopis name for Krishna, meaning 'dark'.

Listen to all, but only others in the circle tell of inner

experiences...

Stay silent and make peace your guide, avoiding ugly

consequences.

Live like this in the ocean of becoming and your heart

commences

by this to be a part of cultivating spiritual wealth He
dispenses.
O Rasakhan, devotedly worship Krishna with all the
senses
as women carry water-jugs, talking, laughing, mind on
steadiness.

Dohas...

I've seen that beauty without end of that enchanting
Shyama...
that young monarch of Braj is in my eyes, soul, heart
forever.

Rasakhan, having seen that One's grace my eyes aren't
mine...
like a bow they are drawn, but like an arrow fly towards
mine.

TUKARAM (1608-1654) Tukaram was a prominent Sant (Saint) and spiritual poet during the Bhakti movement in India. Tukaram was born in the small village of Dehu in the state of Maharashtra to Bolhoba and Kanakai a couple belonging to the lower Sudra class.

His real name was Tukaram Vhilhoba Aambe. He is known as Bhakta Tukaram to southern Indian people. He had two brothers. Despite their lower class status the family was well to do and enjoyed good social standing in the village. Tukaram's troubles started with the illness of his father, due to which he had to start supporting his family at the tender age of thirteen. Shortly after, both his parents died. Tukaram's problems only mounted; death of his family members and economic hardship seemed to plague him.

Tukaram was married twice, his first wife Rakhumabai died in 1602 in her early youth due to starvation during a famine, his second wife Jijabai or Avali as she was called, was much younger than his first had been and had little patience with his devotion and for God and she nagged him continuously. They had three sons: Santu or Mahadev, Vithoba and Narayan.

He dreamt that he was initiated by the Lord Hari (God) Himself, dressed as a Brahman. Tukaram continuously sang the praises of the Lord in the form of *abhangs* which he wrote. These were in his mother tongue Marathi. The hundreds of *abhangs* expressed his feelings and philosophical outlook.

During his 41 years, Tukaram composed over 5,000 *abhangs*. Many of them speak of events in his life, which make them somewhat autobiographical. Yet, they are focused on God, Pandurang, and not Tukaram.

His *abhangs* became very popular with the masses of common people. It was this very popularity that caused the religious establishment (the high caste Brahmins) to hate and persecute Tukaram, as he was causing them to lose their power over the people.

There are many miracles attributed to Tukaram. Tukaram was a devotee of Vitthala or Vithoba, a form of God Vishnu. Tukaram is considered to be the climactic point of a tradition, which is thought to have begun in Maharashtra with Namdev see his section previously). Dnyaneshwar, Janabai, Eknath and Tukaram are revered especially in Maharashtra.

Tukaram was also the subject of a great film, title *Sant Tukaram*, made in 1936 by V. Damle and S. Fattelal of the Prabhat Film Company, Pune, starring Vishnupant Pagnis as the lead and released on December 12, 1936 at the Central Cinema in Mumbai. The film was a big hit and broke all previous records by running continuously for 57 weeks. It also won an award at the 5th Venice International Film Festival in 1937 and still remains a part of film appreciation courses in India. Other films on his life and many recordings have been made.

Further Reading...

The Poems of Tukarama Translated & re-arranged with notes & Introduction by J. Nelson Fraser and K.B. Marathe, Motilal Banarsidass, Delhi, 1909.

Life of Tukaram by Justin E. Abbot, Motilal Banarsidass, Delhi, 1980.

Focus on Tukaram From A Fresh Angle by S. R. Sharma, Popular Book Depot, 1962.

Says Tuka: Selected Poetry of Tukaram, Translated from the Marathi with an Introduction by Dilip Chitre, Penguin Books, New Delhi, 1991.

Inspirations of Saint Tukaram with a short sketch of his life, by P.R. Munge, Self Published, Bombay, 1930.

The Great Integrators: The Saint-Singers of India by Dr. V. Raghavan, Publications Division, Ministry of Information & Broadcasting, New Delhi, 1964, (Pages 136-8).

Minstrels of God, Part 2, by Bankey Behari, Bharatiya Vidya Bhavan, Bombay, 1970. (Pages 260-271).

An Indian Peasant Mystic: Translation from Tukaram by John S. Hoyland, Prinit Press, 1969.

Tukaram by Ramchandra Dattatraya Ranade, S.U.N.Y. Press, New York, 1994.

Tukaram's Teachings by S. R. Sharma, Bharatiya Vidya

Bhavan, Chowpatty, 1964.
Wikipedia Article.

Abhangs...

One knowing a devout heart's love is God's darling.

No other I long for, even if wise and full of learning.

Who fixes mind on God's name, form, I am serving.

Tuka says: he knows nine pure ways of worshipping.

These are not my clothes or my country...

I have wandered here by chance, you see?

What as mine can I be claiming honestly?

Where's there a place to be resting for me?

I call my hands and feet mine dishonestly!

I'm blind and lame and none befriends me.

Lord, help me, no brother or child do I see!

To the saints I commit myself completely.

I shake as I follow the pathway before me.

Ears can hear... what happens I can't see.

At crossroads I sit, thoughts on You only!

Like one losing the way I cry out for mercy.

My belly is never full, feet never rest easy!

I'm tired of walking through villages daily.

Now I stay here, who to trust, you tell me!

Who will bring to me alms, unexpectedly?

I often hear Your praises sung passionately

as I am now singing: O Lord, befriend me!

I am O so hungry, but, You give so freely!

All worthwhile I had I gave up completely.

Wealth, wife, son, mother were left by me.

O Lord, I gave up lust, it was Your decree!

Tuka says: All-powerful You, protect me!

I can't bear to hear to restrain myself, soul is tired:

I can't bear any company, of me only I am pleased.

Of this world of sensuous desires I am exhausted:

Tuka says: lust and illusion kept us from the Lord.

O God, in my hands and feet a cripple am I,

on a self-willed mount I sit as time goes by.

If I spur on, fences, holes... too fast will fly!

I've none to lean on, no father, mother have I.

O you generous people, give me a gift for my

trip to Pandharpura... to get there I now try.

I've gone door to door on my crutches, until I

am so worn away from tiredness I could cry!

None comes to help or save me: in pain am I.
Let God show me power saints tell in a cry!
He in Pandharpura helps cripples, I don't lie!
Due to belly, on this world depending am I.
Crying 'mother, father'... nothing, but I try!
Contempt everywhere, often at me does fly.
No pity, 'Move on,' and dogs to bite me try!
Many strong desires possess me, I could cry.
I don't know what sins I did in time gone by.
I know not my good, bad; no memory have I.
I've lost mind like moth who to burn does try.
Give me my life, O You Who in Life does lie.
I've travelled far, much pain suffered, have I.
This is the reason that I'm here, in You I rely.
To find is hard; I meet You, at Your feet lay I.
I Tuka, fold hands, bow to the saints on high!

My life has passed in every pleasure seeking:
not a moment, liberation I've been pursuing.
I've hurt myself by in all regions wandering:
in the illusion my life I have been shrouding.
None know how I am, myself I am helping!
Even saints source of bliss are not knowing!

How to tell womb's torments I'm enduring?
O Narayana, flesh's fluids I was knowing.
When I tried to think of You, when nearing
was death You were near, I wasn't knowing.
Dust to dust, past's store to soul is clinging!
Now... I beg You, that You I can be serving.
Tuka cries to You Kesava, path be showing!

Singing Your praises makes me so happy,
to tell about Your love tastes sweet to me.
Two birds were born upon only one tree...
coming near was the hunter, them did see.
He let his hawk be flying near to the tree:
then into a bow an arrow he placed firmly.
From this You the birds think of instantly:
"Come, our mother, father, our state see!
If we fly up the hawk sees us, obviously...
if we stay, hunter will shoot us, quickly!"
Hearing birds, a serpent's form took He:
He bit hunter, arrow hit hawk... deadly!
To Your servants You're so full of mercy:
in times of danger You help, we can see.
Tuka says: no words can't tell how happy
You are in these worlds numbering three!

That the world is only God, this may be true,

but what one needs is good advice, I tell you.

First, destroy 'you' and test is gone through!

Treasure of divine knowledge comes to you,

when upon this matter you can advise, too!

Tuka says: this is fifth stage of freeing you,

when into cause the effect is absorbed, too.

Into a trance I have fallen, I run about wildly:

He comes I'm happy, I love Govinda madly!

Now, all begging, crying is given up by me...

at His feet I lay my head in worship, humbly.

Some news of Govinda, someone now tell me:

on shoulder He sat me, now Him I don't see.

When into my head came this pride of beauty?

Compassionate One, I beg You to... me pity!

In the past many lost You through pride, I see:

the same mistake has now been made by me!

When I see You, I am renouncing my body...

the world vanishes and ended is the journey!

If we cry over all we gave up it is obvious we
have committed sin against You, obviously.
I say: if one acts in this way, it is unworthy!
Govinda, Tuka's Lord, I can now clearly see.

Now, no more will I ever be returning...
with that One in love I am now falling.
Can world's anger me now be hurting?
Why are most people always shouting?
All you are strangers to me I'm saying!
You say whatever you may be choosing
but it will be false what you are saying.
Only of meeting Him I am thinking...
to His Form my eyes stay, unblinking.
For a moment Him I can't bear leaving.
Other actions I don't want to be doing.
I'm only happy when Him I'm hearing.
With love's dart my heart He's piercing.
My life away from Him I'd be dreading.
In my mind He is all that is remaining.
I'll never go back, as here I'm staying.
In the future don't you me be loving...
as Tuka's Lord and I are united being.

RAMDAS (1627-1682). Ramdas was a prominent Marathi saint and religious poet in the Hindu tradition in Maharashtra, India; he was a contemporary of Tukaram (see previously). Samarth Ramdas was a devotee of Lord Rama. His birth name was Narayan Suryajipant Kulkarni Thosar.

Ramdas was born in Jalna District of Maharashtra. As a child he showed an inclination toward metaphysical contemplation and religion. When eight his father died and when he was eighteen his mother arranged his marriage. However, he wanted to pursue a monastic life and ran away in the marriage ceremony. The Hindu marriage ceremony's last word that seal the marriage is 'Saavdhan' meaning, 'careful'. Ramdas interpreted it to mean that he had to not get entangled in the bonds of *maya* and must seek Self-realization.

Ramdas moved around a lot and in the process used several small caves for meditation. For the next twelve years he devoted himself to studying religious books, meditation and to prayers in a place named Panchavati, near Nashik on the banks of the Godavari River. At 24 he took the name 'Ramdas', meaning 'servant of Lord Rama,' an Avatar of God.

Ramdas practiced yoga exercises as well as meditation. In addition to his veneration of Rama, Ramdas worshipped Rama's divinely strong servant Lord Hanuman (i.e. Universal Mind). He established temples of Hanuman in Maharashtra and promoted physical exercise to develop a healthy society.

Like the Perfect Master Tukaram he was connected spiritually and visited the great Perfect Master and the Leader/Conqueror of Maharashtra, the great Shivaji.

Ramdas was a gifted poet. He produced considerable poetry in Marathi. Among his works, two compositions stand out: a small book of meditations *Shri Manache Slok* couplets on ethical behaviour and love for God (see following), and a large volume, *Dasbodh,* his masterpiece.

Ramdas' ways were peculiar. He appeared to the outside world as a mad man. He had a small bow. He used to have, by his side, a large number of stones with which he pelted every object he saw. Ramdas had eleven hundred disciples of whom three hundred were women.

This great Perfect Master (Qutub or Sadguru) of Maharashtra breathed his last in 1682 at Sajjangad, near Satara, a fortress that was given to him by Shivaji for his residence. At the time of his departure from the world it is said a dazzling light emanated from his body and Ramdas was absorbed in the image of his Lord, Avatar Rama.

Further Reading...

Spiritual Treasure of Saint Ramadasa by V.H. Date, Motilal Banarsidass, Delhi, 1975.
Ramdas: Translated from Mahipati's Santavijaya by Justin E. Abbot, Poona City, 1932.
Shri Samartha Ramdas, by Prem Lata, Ess Ess Publishers , New Delhi, 1991.
'O Mind': Insight into Samartha Ramdas Swamy's 'Manache Shlika' by Arun Godbole, Motilal Banarsidass, New Delhi, 2002.
Dasboadh of Samarth Ramdas, by Diwakar Ghaisas, Keshav Bhikaji Dhawale, 2012.
The Life and Mission of Samarth Ramdas by K.S. Thackeray, University of Michigan Library, 1918.
Dasbodh, an English version, an elixir of human excellence: A treatise in Marathi of Shri Samartha Ramdas Swami, a great motivator saint, Shri Samarth Ramdas Swami Krupa Trust, 1991.
Verses Addressed To The Mind (Manache Shlok By Sant Samartha Ramdas) Translated by Swami Chidananda, Divine Life Society Pub. 2006.
Stories of Indian Saints Translation of Mahipati's Marathi Bhaktavijaya, by Justin E. Abbot & Narhar R. Godbole, Motilal Banarsidass, Delhi, 1933.
Sufis, Mystics and Yogis of India by Bankey Behari, Bharatiya Vidya Bhavan, Bombay, 1962.
Mysticism in Maharashtra by R.D. Ranade, Motilal Banarsidass, Delhi, 1933.

Saints of Maharashtra by Savitribai Khanolkar, Bharatiya Vidya Bhavan, Bombay, 1990.
The Great Integrators: The Saint-Singers of India by Dr. V. Raghavan, Publications Division, New Delhi 1974.
Wikipedia Article.

Slokas from 'Manache Slok'
(Couplets addressed to the Mind).

Bhakti is the only way God that Himself is revealing...

one has to also live a life morally, all sins to be avoiding.

One who has good morals is blessed, to God devoted...

in the early hours of morning on Him he has meditated.

Don't hold onto evil thoughts, let the mind be set upon

what's essential and lasts, that is... His Name rest on.

All thoughts about the sensuous life, be giving away...

get stuck on what is true now and eternally, every day.

If you should become angry, later you'll be repenting...

give up hydra-headed desire, jealousy, prideful acting!

With extraordinary courage take insults thrown at you:

only speak sweet words, humbly, they'll soon love you!

Act in such a way, after you die others will pay respect:

saints are pleased if like sandlewood you've good effect.

Don't eye others riches or you will be committing a sin

that comes back on you... unhappiness will then begin.

Forget all body's pleasures and fix mind on Rama only:
then you'll know even body's pain won't stop divinity!

In this world is not a one who is happy in every way...
look, you'll find that all reap what they sow, each day!
Do not let your mind be affected by grief and anxiety:
don't think of the body, and while living you'll be free!
Be in a hurry to get far from the mind's crookedness...
death will come: Ravana*lost all from his sinfulness!
No matter the *karma* due to all, in this world born...
all, great or small, must into death's jaws go, I warn!
One thinks of greatness, not death, from ignorance...
ah, one has to leave all and die, this is true... confess!
One dies, another mourns but soon has to die also...
one's greed keeps one miserable, to birth again to go.
One's anxiety's useless, all as the result of previous
actions happens: not knowing one's getting nervous.
Why sing of mankind's glory? Sing... of Lord Rama!
Vedas... Puranas praise Him. Bring on good *karma!*
Do not leave the Truth's path for that of falseness...
speak only the truth for a lie stays a lie, this I stress!
I wish mind was free of desire for wealth and women:

then I may realize God and round of births abandon.
Each hour, nearer and nearer your death is coming...
at death only God helps: Rama's name be repeating!

Why waste life, and like the ordinary people, grieve?
Take God's name always and all your sinning leave.
Rama's vision's guaranteed in future like happiness?
Listen... all but God and His Name is nothingness!
Try to stay healthy, death will take it away finally...
love Rama, about what happens to life don't worry.
Give up fear of the world, Lord Rama protects you:
He will protect you even though Death is after you.
Keep this truth: Rama is proud of you... is merciful!
The bow's in His hand, so Death of fear is now full.
Are any in the world wary or angry with one who is
a servant of Rama Who always protecting them is?
Rama loves His devotees, *Puranas* tell us that He
bears their burdens, but mankind acts unfaithfully.
How God treats us on we treat Him is depending:
if we place our faith in Him, He... us is protecting.
Rama's bliss incarnate, to lovers He's indifferent?
He only wishes they will be brave, not indifferent.
He isn't indifferent, saving them from calamities:

He's like rising sun, removing morning birds cries!
Mind of mine, I pray to you to in Rama be stuck...
to look at that One with joy and to be awestruck!

Live in Rama Who the *Vedas* and *Puranas* praise:
be content to at His feet offer all your fickle ways.
Live in Rama and see Him with reverence, clearly:
you will banish evil thoughts, experience divinity.
Do not wander aimlessly, it is useless, tiring too:
to stay with Rama's always the right thing to do.
Know this: be friends with Rama, with Him live.
You'll then hear His anklets, He to you will give.
Always meditate upon His Name so you will be
given grace: say not a word, not about His glory.
Don't talk to people, Name of Rama only say...
leave where it isn't said, in forest it joyfully say.
Where He can't be meditated on is nowhere to be:
there only selfishness is, there ends all spirituality.
Awake, aware one gazes closely at Rama's vision:
that one knows time without Rama is not for one.
Among Rama's servants blessed is who is seeing
with physical eyes Rama inside... Him glorifying:
also, who doesn't spare body in promoting Rama,

doing duties, faithfully… saying Name of Rama.
Rama's servant's blessed who does what he says,
worshipping the one Deity, and no doubt is his…

and Rama's servant is blessed who lust gives up,
who is celibate, no pain, pleasure, mind grown-up!
Blessed is one who leaves jealousy, selfishness…
world's things; who, still speaks with sweetness.
Blessed is one who meditates, with others talking
of Reality, and never being arrogant and arguing.
Blessed is Rama's servant who's straightforward,
who is truthful, and all love that one… in accord!
Rama's servant's blessed who to Him is faithful
always: not fanciful, meditates in forest until full.
Rama's servant is blessed who Rama his debtor
from his love for Him, always His thirsty lover.
Rama's servant is blessed, who helps the needy,
and wretched: can that one's mind become angry?
Bless your life by on Rama's Name meditating,
you will be free from all inhibitions, all worrying.
If you want to meditate on Rama have no desire:
desire means sin, to meet Him you must be pure!

BAHINA BAI (1628-1700). Bahina Bai or Bahinabai is a Varkari female-saint from Maharashtra, India. She is considered as a disciple of another Varkari poet-saint Tukaram (see his section previously). Born in a brahmin family, Bahinabai was married to a widower at a tender age and spent most of her childhood wandering around Maharashtra along with her family. She describes, in her autobiography *Atmamanivedana*, her spiritual experiences with a calf and visions of the Varkari's patron deity Vithoba and Tukaram. She reports being subjected to verbal and physical abuse by her husband who despised her spiritual inclination but who finally accepted her chosen path of devotion (*bhakti*). Unlike most female-saints who never married or renounced their married life for God, she remained married her entire life.

Bahina Bai's *abhangs* written in Marathi also focus on her troubled marital life and the regret being born a woman. Bahina Bai was always torn between her duties to her husband and her devotion to Vithoba. Her poetry mirrors her compromise between her devotion to her husband and God.

In Kolhapur she was exposed to Hari-Kirtana songs and

tales from the scripture, the *Bhagavata Purana*. She began to have visions. In these visions Tukaram fed her nectar and taught her the mantra 'Rama-Krishna-Hari'. Soon Bahina Bai pronounced Tukaram as her Spiritual Master or *guru*. In her visions Tukaram initiated her into the path of *bhakti* (love, devotion) and instructed her to recite the name of Vithoba. Some people considered her behaviour as a sign of madness, while others considered it a mark of sainthood.

As her fame spread her husband was jealous of the attention she received. He is reported to have abused, beaten and confined her to the cattle-shed. When all methods fail to deter her he decided to leave her, she was three months pregnant at the time. However, he could not do it as he suffered a burning limbs sensation lasting a month on the day of departure. Finally he repented and was convinced of Bahina Bai's faith and devotion to God. At the same time, she realized her neglect of her husband and decided to stay with him.

The family went to Dehu the home-town of Tukaram and paid their respects to him. Here, the brahmin Bahina Bai's acceptance of the lower caste Sudra Tukaram as her *guru* agitated local brahmins which led to harassment of the family and threatening of ostracism.

In Dehu Bahina Bai gave birth to a daughter who she

named Kasibai. But, she was distressed and mediated suicide. Tukaram in a vision stopped her and blessed her with poetic powers and prophesied that she would have a son who was a companion in her previous birth... so Bahina Bai is believed to have started composition of poetry, the first of which were dedicated to Vithoba. She had a son who she named Vithoba.

Finally the family moved to Shirur where Bahina Bai practiced a vow of silence for a while.

In 1649, on Tukaram's death, Bahina Bai revisited Dehu and fasted for eighteen days where, according to the traditional account, she was blessed with a vision of Tukaram again.

She then visited the saint/poet Ramdas (see his section previously) and stayed in his company until his death in 1682. Afterwards she returned to Shirur.

In last sections of her autobiography she says she has 'seen her death'. She prophesied her death and wrote a letter to her son who had gone to Shukeshwar to perform last rites of his wife. On her death-bed, Bahina Bai told Vithoba that he had been her son throughout her twelve previous births and also in her current birth, which she believed was her last. Apart from her autobiography Bahina Bai composed *abhangs* which deal with various subjects like praise of Vithoba, Atman, the Sadguru (Perfect Master or *Qutub*), sainthood and devotion.

She has also composed a text called *Pundalika-Mahatmya,* which details the legend of Vithoba and devotee Pundalik, a central figure in Varkari tradition.

Further Reading...

Bahina Bai: A Translation of Her Autobiography and Verses by Justin E. Abbott, Motilal Banarsidass, Delhi, 1929.
Bahinabai: by Jesse Russell & Ronald Cohn, Books on Demand Ltd, 2012.
Bahina Bai and Her Abhangs: Translated into English Verse with an Introduction by Krishna P. Bahadur, Munshiram Manoharial Publishers Pvt. Ltd. New Delhi, 1998.
Stories of Indian Saints Translation of Mahipati's Marathi Bhaktavijaya, by Justin E. Abbot & Narhar R. Godbole, Motilal Banarsidass, Delhi, 1933.
Mysticism in Maharashtra by R.D. Ranade, Motilal Banarsidass, Delhi, 1933.
Saints of Maharashtra by Savitribai Khanolkar, Bharatiya Vidya Bhavan, Bombay, 1990.
Wikipedia Article.

Abhangs...

With all my heart I'll to Guru's feet be clinging:
without end, that One I will be contemplating!
If I do this, my heart, what will you be having?
In the net of thinking yourself you'll be finding.
My trust in the Guru's words I will be placing:
for that One I have a love that won't be dying.
My true Guru I'll always be a slave, serving...
I will never of any worldly desires, be thinking!
At His feet I'll offer body, heart, all speaking:
in this heart my perfect Guru, I'll be keeping!
Bahini: rid heart of self and Guru be begging!

Heart, desire for worldly things in an earlier birth was
formed;
so... inside you power of such worldly things in you is
unconquered.
And so, I say this, that I pray that by you I should be

listened:

all sensual organs I have to be obedient to me... now
caused.

If I can reveal to you... of my body nothing will have
stayed:

I'll fast, not breathe, in hottest season I will in fire be
seated.

I'll torture body by open fire hanging down into it my
head:

I'll wander across all of the earth to all places that are
sacred.

To practise yoga I'll sit and contemplate, and I'll fast
unaided!

I'll let my body be sawn to bits, so... what'll you have
gained?

Bahini says: O heart, do what I say, if not be begging
instead.

Who ever takes right-thinking as a companion,

whatever holds up that one's sinning is broken.

Right-thinking has now by me as helper taken;

so... heart, of you I'll not worry or be mistaken.

If right-thinking is united to detachment, then

of right-thinking *bhakti* is the servant... again.
Bahini says: right-thinking is the true friend...
and so who now needs to pay to you attention?

One, who always sings God's praises and is repeating
His attributes, is one as one of *bhakti* I'd be describing.
No time passes without that one His name repeating:
no time is passing when that one *bhakti* is not craving.
That one's eyes see God, that one's lips are praising...
to *shastras** telling of freedom, ears keep on listening;
hands are serving and feet around His image walking:
this is the path to attain peace, and soul to be resting.
This happens all the hours of the day without ceasing,
in the homes of saints in their attitude... unassuming.
Bahini says: *bhakti* is the one that salvation is giving,
but it comes with one to be the saints humbly serving.

> *Bhakti,* is the highest way to salvation...
> through it, into one's hand... lies heaven.
> Let heart be strong and love be unbroken:
> then, you will arrive at Vishnu's heaven.
> *Bhakti's* servants are detachment driven:
> before *bhakti* all other means are hidden.

Bahini: *bhakti* is detachment, going on...
allow your heart to think upon this again.

Without *bhakti* one's life is not worth living...
all that life means to that one, is disappearing.
Why look at him, why was mother life giving?
That one, any of the saints is not respecting...
and that one, to the scriptures is not listening!
Bahini says: one, who to God is not praying,
can that one... a detached heart be acquiring?

One doesn't need to read the *Shastras* or the *Vedas;* *
by a very different means one obtains spiritual riches.
With heart's feelings go to true Guru on your knees...
you will become like God, as one of the consequences.
One does not need rites or ceremonies or austerities...
ways of having a spiritual life are different from these.
One needs not idols, sacred sites or any pilgrimages...
better to search through mystic couplets of the *Vedas*.
There is no need for yoga, breath control or sacrifices:
the secret way to be discovering it is in none of these.
One does not need to be chaste or one who marries...

or anyone who gives up all worldly things that please.

Without value are all kinds of religious ceremonies...

including, on fire sucking smoke, five-fire austerities.

Bahini: deliverance only through a true Guru comes;

and, not by any naked yogi living in the wilderness!

When washed away disappear may blackness, whiteness:

but, can fire ever its burning nature even try to suppress?

Also, Fate will never be forsaking one, not more or less...

and even the head of any wise man can come under stress.

And can water ever give up its characteristic of coolness:

then would anyone expect mind to give up its fickleness?

Bahini says: the question is answered, cleared this mess,

when finally upon the feet of the perfect Guru one gazes!

Earth, water, and light and air and ether...

these natural elements in this universe are.

Taking bits He made things, was Namer:

so us for our best on earth, He... our saver.

Bones, flesh and skin and veins and hair...

special five from element earth... together.
Saliva, urine, semen, sweat, blood, five are
that He created from the element... water.
Coitus, thirst, sleep, laziness, and hunger,
the five, taken from the element light, are.
To move, turn, stop, contract, go; together
are taken from the element known as 'air'.
Shame, temptation, hatred, anger, fear...
in these five elements... the qualities are.
So characteristics of five, twenty-five are:
with much effort He brought all together.
Law: hundred years of life He was maker;
with three qualities, them was connector.
Four *Vedas* as oarsmen appointed were...
then to God a sacrifice was given... later.
Bahini says: God created the Name as a
boat to save all... as we ocean cross over.

Everyone is now acting as a guru and is preaching...
but none know the worth of the true Guru's helping.
About many kinds of knowledge they go on talking;
meditation, austerities, names of God be repeating,
but... character of the true Guru they aren't having.

Authority of *Vedas* and *Shastras* they are claiming:
all professors of high powers God will be punishing.
Mantras, prayers, magic mysteries they'll be giving:
like this, none to feet of true Guru, will be reaching.
Bahini says: why vainly for one's body go on caring?
Worship at true Guru's feet, all… there be finding!

BOOKS PUBLISHED BY NEW HUMANITY BOOKS BOOK HEAVEN

*Most 6" x 9" (15 cm x 23 cm) Paperbacks Perfectbound
unless stated otherwise...
Most also available in pdf format
from: www.newhumanitybooksbookheaven.com
check out our website for prices & full descriptions of each book.
Also available from Amazon.com
many titles are also in Kindle format e-books*

TRANSLATIONS

*(NOTE: All translations by Paul Smith are in clear, modern English
and in the correct rhyme-structure of the originals and as close to the
true meaning as possible.)*

DIVAN OF HAFIZ
Revised Translation & Introduction by Paul Smith
This is a completely revised one volume edition of the only modern,
poetic version of Hafiz's masterpiece of 791 *ghazals, masnavis,
rubais* and other poems/songs. The spiritual and historical and
human content is here in understandable, beautiful poetry: the
correct rhyme-structure has been achieved, without intruding, in
readable (and singable) English. In the Introduction of 70 pages his
life story is told in greater detail than any where else; his spirituality
is explored, his influence on the life, poetry and art of the East and
the West, the form and function of his poetry, and the use of his book
as a worldly guide and spiritual oracle. His Book, like the *I Ching*, is
one of the world's Great Oracles. Included are notes to most poems,
glossary and selected bibliography and two indexes. First published
in a two-volume hardback limited edition in 1986 the book quickly
went out of print. 542 pages.

PERSIAN AND HAFIZ SCHOLARS AND ACADEMICS WHO HAVE
COMMENTED ON PAUL SMITH'S TRANSLATION OF HAFIZ'S
'DIVAN'.
"It is not a joke... the English version of ALL the *ghazals* of Hafiz is
a great feat and of paramount importance. I am astonished. If he
comes to Iran I will kiss the fingertips that wrote such a masterpiece
inspired by the Creator of all and I will lay down my head at his feet
out of respect." Dr. Mir Mohammad Taghavi (Dr. of Literature)
Tehran.
"I have never seen such a good translation and I would like to write a
book in Farsi and introduce his Introduction to Iranians." Mr B.
Khorramshai, Academy of Philosophy, Tehran.
"Superb translations. 99% Hafiz 1% Paul Smith."Ali Akbar
Shapurzman, translator of many mystical works in English to
Persian and knower of Hafiz's *Divan* off by heart.
"I was very impressed with the beauty of these books." Dr. R.K.
Barz. Faculty of Asian Studies, Australian National University.
"Smith has probably put together the greatest collection of literary
facts and history concerning Hafiz." Daniel Ladinsky (Penguin
Books author of poems inspired by Hafiz).

HAFIZ – THE ORACLE
(For Lovers, Seekers, Pilgrims, and the God-Intoxicated).
Translation & Introduction by Paul Smith. 441 pages.

HAFIZ OF SHIRAZ.
The Life, Poetry and Times of the Immortal Persian Poet.
In Three Books by Paul Smith. Over 1900 pages, 3 volumes.

PIERCING PEARLS: THE COMPLETE ANTHOLOGY
OF PERSIAN POETRY
(Court, Sufi, Dervish, Satirical, Ribald, Prison & Social Poetry
from the 9th to the 20th century.) Volume One
Translations, Introduction and Notes by Paul Smith. Pages 528.

PIERCING PEARLS: THE COMPLETE ANTHOLOGY
OF PERSIAN POETRY

(Court, Sufi, Dervish, Satirical, Ribald, Prison & Social Poetry from the 9th to the 20th century.) Vol. Two
Translations, Introduction and Notes by Paul Smith. Pages 462.

DIVAN OF SADI: His Mystical Love-Poetry.
Translation & Introduction by Paul Smith. 421 pages.

RUBA'IYAT OF SADI
Translation & Introduction by Paul Smith. 151 pages.

WINE, BLOOD & ROSES:
ANTHOLOGY OF TURKISH POETS
Sufi, Dervish, Divan, Court & Folk Poetry from the 12th – 20th Century
Translations, Introductions, Notes etc., by Paul Smith. Pages 286.

OBEYD ZAKANI: THE DERVISH JOKER.
A Selection of his Poetry, Prose, Satire, Jokes and Ribaldry.
Translation & Introduction by Paul Smith. 305 pages.

OBEYD ZAKANI'S > MOUSE & CAT ^ ^
(The Ultimate Edition)
Translation & Introduction etc by Paul Smith. 191 pages.

THE GHAZAL: A WORLD ANTHOLOGY
Translations, Introductions, Notes, Etc. by Paul Smith. Pages 658.

NIZAMI: THE TREASURY OF MYSTERIES
Translation & Introduction by Paul Smith. 251 pages.

NIZAMI: LAYLA AND MAJNUN
Translation & Introduction by Paul Smith. 215 pages.

UNITY IN DIVERSITY
Anthology of Sufi and Dervish Poets of the Indian Sub-Continent
Translations, Introductions, Notes, Etc. by Paul Smith. Pages... 356.

RUBA'IYAT OF RUMI
Translation & Introduction and Notes by Paul Smith. 367 pages.

THE *MASNAVI*: A WORLD ANTHOLOGY
Translations, Introduction and Notes by Paul Smith. 498 pages.

HAFIZ'S FRIEND, JAHAN KHATUN:
The Persian Princess Dervish Poet...
A Selection of Poems from her *Divan*
Translated by Paul Smith with Rezvaneh Pashai. 267 pages.

PRINCESSES, SUFIS, DERVISHES, MARTYRS &
FEMINISTS: NINE GREAT WOMEN POETS OF THE
EAST: A Selection of the Poetry of Rabi'a of Basra, Rabi'a of
Balkh, Mahsati, Lalla Ded, Jahan Khatun, Makhfi, Tahirah,
Hayati and Parvin.
Translation & Introduction by Paul Smith. Pages 367.

RUMI: SELECTED POEMS
Translation, Introduction & Notes by Paul Smith. 220 pages.

KABIR: SEVEN HUNDRED SAYINGS *(SAKHIS)*.
Translation & Introduction by Paul Smith. 190 pages. Third Edition

SHAH LATIF: SELECTED POEMS
Translation & Introduction by Paul Smith. 172 pages

LALLA DED: SELECTED POEMS
Translation & Introduction by Paul Smith. 140 pages.

BULLEH SHAH: SELECTED POEMS
Translation & Introduction by Paul Smith. 141 pages.

NIZAMI: MAXIMS
Translation & Introduction Paul Smith. 214 pages.

KHIDR IN SUFI POETRY: A SELECTION

Translation & Introduction by Paul Smith. 267 pages.

ADAM: THE FIRST PERFECT MASTER AND POET
by Paul Smith. 222 pages.

MODERN SUFI POETRY: A SELECTION
Translations & Introduction by Paul Smith. Pages 249

LIFE, TIMES & POETRY OF NIZAMI
by Paul Smith. 97 pages.

RABI'A OF BASRA: SELECTED POEMS
Translation by Paul Smith. 102 pages.

RABI'A OF BASRA & MANSUR HALLAJ
~Selected Poems~
Translation & Introduction Paul Smith. Pages 134

SATIRICAL PROSE OF OBEYD ZAKANI
Translation and Introduction by Paul Smith. 212 pages.

KHAQANI: SELECTED POEMS
Translation & Introduction by Paul Smith. 197 pages.

IBN 'ARABI: SELECTED POEMS
Translation & Introduction by Paul Smith. 121 pages.

THE *GHAZAL* IN SUFI & DERVISH POETRY:
An Anthology:
Translations, Introductions, by Paul Smith Pages 548.

A GREAT TREASURY OF POEMS
BY GOD-REALIZED & GOD-INTOXICATED POETS
Translation & Introduction by Paul Smith. Pages 804.

MAKHFI: THE PRINCESS SUFI POET ZEB-UN-NISSA
A Selection of Poems from her *Divan*

Translation & Introduction by Paul Smith. 154 pages.

~ THE SUFI RUBA'IYAT ~
A Treasury of Sufi and Dervish Poetry in the *Ruba'i* form,
from Rudaki to the 21st Century
Translations, Introductions, by Paul Smith. Pages... 304.

LOVE'S AGONY & BLISS: ANTHOLOGY OF URDU
POETRY: Sufi, Dervish, Court and Social Poetry from the 16th- 20th
Century
Translations, Introductions, Etc. by Paul Smith. Pages 298.

RUBA'IYAT OF ANSARI
Translation & Introduction by Paul Smith. 183 pages

THE RUBAI'YAT: A WORLD ANTHOLOGY:
Court, Sufi, Dervish, Satirical, Ribald, Prison and Social Poetry in
the *Ruba'i* form from the 9th to the 20th century from the Arabic,
Persian, Turkish, Urdu and English.
Translations, Introduction and Notes by Paul Smith Pages 388.

BREEZES OF TRUTH
Selected Early & Classical Arabic Sufi Poetry
Translations, Introductions by Paul Smith. Pages 248.

THE~DIVINE~WINE:
A Treasury of Sufi and Dervish Poetry (Volume One)
Translations, Introductions by Paul Smith. Pages... 522.

THE~DIVINE~WINE:
A Treasury of Sufi and Dervish Poetry (Volume Two)
Translations, Introductions by Paul Smith. Pages... 533.

TONGUES ON FIRE: An Anthology of the Sufi, Dervish,
Warrior & Court Poetry of Afghanistan.
Translations, Introductions, Etc. by Paul Smith. 322 pages.

THE SEVEN GOLDEN ODES (QASIDAS) OF ARABIA
(The Mu'allaqat)
Translations, Introduction & Notes by Paul Smith. Pages... 147.

THE QASIDA: A WORLD ANTHOLOGY
Translations, Introduction & Notes by Paul Smith. Pages... 354.

IBN AL-FARID: WINE & THE MYSTIC'S PROGRESS
Translation, Introduction & Notes by Paul Smith. 174 pages.

RUBA'IYAT OF ABU SA'ID
Translation, Introduction & Notes by Paul Smith. 227 pages.

RUBA'IYAT OF BABA TAHIR
Translations, Introduction & Notes by Paul Smith. 154 pages.

THE POETS OF SHIRAZ
Sufi, Dervish, Court & Satirical Poets from the 9th to the 20th
Centuries of the fabled City of Shiraz .
Translations & Introduction & Notes by Paul Smith. 428 pages.

RUBA'IYAT OF 'ATTAR
Translation, Introduction & Notes by Paul Smith. 138 Pages.

RUBA'IYAT OF MAHSATI
Translation, Introduction & Notes by Paul Smith. 150 Pages.

RUBA'IYAT OF JAHAN KHATUN
Translation by Paul Smith with Rezvaneh Pashai
Introduction & Notes by Paul Smith. 157 Pages.

RUBA'IYAT OF SANA'I
Translation, Introduction & Notes by Paul Smith. 129 Pages.

RUBA'IYAT OF JAMI
Translation, Introduction & Notes by Paul Smith. 179 Pages.

RUBA'IYAT OF SARMAD
Translation, Introduction & Notes by Paul Smith. 381 pages.

RUBA'IYAT OF HAFIZ
Translation, Introduction & Notes by Paul Smith. 221 Pages.

GREAT SUFI POETS OF THE PUNJAB & SINDH:
AN ANTHOLOGY
Translations & Introductions by Paul Smith 166 pages.

YUNUS EMRE, THE TURKISH DERVISH:
SELECTED POEMS
Translation, Introduction & Notes by Paul Smith. Pages 237.

RUBA'IYAT OF KAMAL AD-DIN
Translation, Introduction & Notes by Paul Smith. Pages 170.

RUBA'YAT OF KHAYYAM
Translation, Introduction & Notes by Paul Smith
Reprint of 1909 Introduction by R.A. Nicholson. 268 pages.

RUBA'IYAT OF AUHAD UD-DIN
Translation and Introduction by Paul Smith. 127 pages.

RUBA'IYAT OF AL-MA'ARRI
Translation & Introduction by Paul Smith. 151 pages

ANTHOLOGY OF CLASSICAL ARABIC POETRY
(From Pre-Islamic Times to Al-Shushtari)
Translations, Introduction and Notes by Paul Smith. Pages 287.

THE QIT'A
Anthology of the 'Fragment' in Arabic, Persian and Eastern Poetry.
Translations, Introduction and Notes by Paul Smith. Pages 423.

HEARTS WITH WINGS
Anthology of Persian Sufi and Dervish Poetry
Translations, Introductions, Etc., by Paul Smith. Pages 623.

HAFIZ: SELECTED POEMS
Translation, Introduction & Notes by Paul Smith. 227 Pages.

'ATTAR: SELECTED POETRY
Translation, Introduction & Notes by Paul Smith. 222 pages.

SANA'I : SELECTED POEMS
Translation, Introduction & Notes by Paul Smith. 148 Pages.

THE ROSE GARDEN OF MYSTERY: SHABISTARI
Translation by Paul Smith.
Introduction by E.H. Whinfield & Paul Smith. Pages 182.

RUDAKI: SELECTED POEMS
Translation, Introduction & Notes by Paul Smith. 142 pages.

SADI: SELECTED POEMS
Translation, Introduction & Notes by Paul Smith. 207 pages.

JAMI: SELECTED POEMS
Translation, Introduction by Paul Smith. 183 Pages.

NIZAMI: SELECTED POEMS
Translation & Introduction by Paul Smith. 235 pages.

RUBA'IYAT OF BEDIL
Translation & Introduction by Paul Smith. 154 pages.

BEDIL: SELECTED POEMS
Translation & Introduction by Paul Smith. Pages... 147.

ANVARI: SELECTED POEMS
Translation & Introduction by Paul Smith. 164 pages.

RUBA'IYAT OF 'IRAQI
Translation & Introduction by Paul Smith. 138 pages.

THE WISDOM OF IBN YAMIN: SELECTED POEMS
Translation & Introduction Paul Smith. 155 pages.

NESIMI: SELECTED POEMS
Translation & Introduction by Paul Smith. 169 pages.

SHAH NI'TMATULLAH: SELECTED POEMS
Translation & Introduction by Paul Smith. 168 pages.

AMIR KHUSRAU: SELECTED POEMS
Translation & Introduction by Paul Smith. 201 pages.

A WEALTH OF POETS:
Persian Poetry at the Courts of Sultan Mahmud in Ghazneh
& Sultan Sanjar in Ganjeh (998-1158)
Translations, Introduction and Notes by Paul Smith. Pages 264.

SHIMMERING JEWELS: Anthology of Poetry Under the Reigns
of the Mughal Emperors of India (1526-1857)
Translations, Introductions, Etc. by Paul Smith. Pages 463.

RAHMAN BABA: SELECTED POEMS
Translation & Introduction by Paul Smith. 141 pages.

RUBA'IYAT OF DARA SHIKOH
Translation & Introduction by Paul Smith. 148 pages.

ANTHOLOGY OF POETRY OF THE CHISHTI SUFI
ORDER Translations & Introduction by Paul Smith. Pages 313.

POEMS OF MAJNUN
Translation & Introduction by Paul Smith. 220 pages.

RUBA'IYAT OF SHAH NI'MATULLAH
Translation & Introduction by Paul Smith. 125 pages.

ANSARI: SELECTED POEMS
Translation & Introduction by Paul Smith. 156 pages.

BABA FARID: SELECTED POEMS
Translation & Introduction by Paul Smith. 164 pages.

POETS OF THE NI'MATULLAH SUFI ORDER
Translations & Introduction by Paul Smith. 244 pages.

MU'IN UD-DIN CHISHTI: SELECTED POEMS
Translation & Introduction by Paul Smith. 171 pages.

QASIDAH BURDAH:
THE THREE POEMS OF THE PROPHET'S MANTLE
Translations & Introduction by Paul Smith. Pages 116.

KHUSHAL KHAN KHATTAK: THE GREAT POET
& WARRIOR OF AFGHANISTAN, SELECTED POEMS
Translation & Introduction by Paul Smith. Pages 187.

RUBA'IYAT OF ANVARI
Translation & Introduction by Paul Smith. 104 pages.

'IRAQI: SELECTED POEMS
Translation & Introduction by Paul Smith. 156 pages.

MANSUR HALLAJ: SELECTED POEMS
Translation & Introduction by Paul Smith. Pages 178.

RUBA'IYAT OF BABA AFZAL
Translation & Introduction by Paul Smith. 178 pages.

RUMI: SELECTIONS FROM HIS *MASNAVI*
Translation & Introduction by Paul Smith. 260 pages.

WINE OF LOVE: AN ANTHOLOGY,
Wine in the Poetry of Arabia, Persia, Turkey &
the Indian Sub-Continent from Pre-Islamic Times to the Present
Translations & Introduction by Paul Smith. 645 pages.

GHALIB: SELECTED POEMS
Translation & Introduction by Paul Smith. Pages 200.

THE ENLIGHTENED SAYINGS OF HAZRAT 'ALI
The Right Hand of the Prophet
Translation & Introduction by Paul Smith. Pages 260.

HAFIZ: TONGUE OF THE HIDDEN
A Selection of *Ghazals* from his *Divan*
Translation & Introduction Paul Smith. 133 pages. Third Edition.

~ HAFIZ: A DAYBOOK ~
Translation & Introduction by Paul Smith. 375 pages.

~˙RUMI˙~ A Daybook
Translation & Introduction by Paul Smith. Pages 383.

SUFI POETRY OF INDIA ~ A Daybook~
Translation & Introduction by Paul Smith. Pages 404.

~ SUFI POETRY~ A Daybook
Translation & Introduction by Paul Smith. Pages 390.

~˙KABIR˙~ A Daybook
Translation & Introduction by Paul Smith. 382 pages.

~ABU SA'ID & SARMAD~ A Sufi Daybook
Translation & Introduction by Paul Smith. 390 pages.

~˙SADI˙~ A Daybook
Translation & Introduction by Paul Smith. 394 pages.

NIZAMI, KHAYYAM & 'IRAQI ... A Daybook
Translation & Introduction by Paul Smith. 380 pages.

ARABIC & AFGHAN SUFI POETRY ... A Daybook
Translation & Introduction by Paul Smith. 392 pages.

TURKISH & URDU SUFI POETS... A Daybook
Translation & Introduction by Paul Smith. 394 pages.

SUFI & DERVISH RUBA'IYAT (9th – 14th century) A
DAYBOOK
Translation & Introduction by Paul Smith. 394 pages.

SUFI & DERVISH RUBA'IYAT (14thth – 20th century)
A DAYBOOK
Translation & Introduction by Paul Smith. 394 pages.

~SAYINGS OF THE BUDDHA: A DAYBOOK~
Revised Translation by Paul Smith from F. Max Muller's. 379
pages.

GREAT WOMEN MYSTICAL POETS OF THE EAST
~ A Daybook ~
Translation & Introduction by Paul Smith. 385 pages.

'ABU NUWAS' SELECTED POEMS
Translation & Introduction by Paul Smith. 154 pages.

HAFIZ: THE SUN OF SHIRAZ:
Essays, Talks, Projects on the Immortal Poet
by Paul Smith. 249 pages.

~'NAZIR AKBARABADI'~ SELECTED POEMS
Translation and Introduction Paul Smith. 191 pages.

'~RUBA'IYAT OF IQBAL~'
Translation & Introduction by Paul Smith. 175 pages.

~'IQBAL'~ SELECTED POETRY
Translation & Introduction by Paul Smith. 183 pages.

>THE POETRY OF INDIA<
Anthology of Poets of India from 3500 B.C. to the 20th century
Translations, Introductions... Paul Smith. Pages... 622.

BHAKTI POETRY OF INDIA... AN ANTHOLOGY
Translations & Introductions Paul Smith. Pages 236.

SAYINGS OF KRISHNA: A DAYBOOK
Translation & Introduction Paul Smith. Pages 376.

~CLASSIC POETRY OF AZERBAIJAN~ An Anthology~
Translation & Introduction Paul Smith. 231 pages.

THE TAWASIN: MANSUR HALLAJ
(Book of the Purity of the Glory of the One)
Translation & Introduction Paul Smith. Pages 264.

MOHAMMED In Arabic, Sufi & Eastern Poetry
Translation & Introduction by Paul Smith. Pages 245.

GITA GOVINDA
The Dance of Divine Love of Radha & Krishna
>Jayadeva< Translation by Puran Singh & Paul Smith. Pages 107.

GREAT WOMEN MYSTICAL POETS OF THE EAST
~ A Daybook ~
Translation & Introduction by Paul Smith. 385 pages.

~SUFI LOVE POETRY~ An Anthology
Translation & Introduction Paul Smith. Pages 560.

HUMA: SELECTED POEMS OF MEHER BABA
Translation & Introduction Paul Smith. Pages 244.

RIBALD POEMS OF THE SUFI POETS
Abu Nuwas, Sana'i, Anvari, Mahsati, Rumi, Sadi and Obeyd
Zakani ... Translation & Introduction Paul Smith. 206 pages.

FIVE GREAT EARLY SUFI MASTER POETS
Mansur Hallaj, Baba Tahir, Abu Sa'id, Ansari & Sana'i
SELECTED POEMS
Translation & Introduction by Paul Smith. Pages 617

FIVE GREAT CLASSIC SUFI MASTER POETS
Khaqani, Mu'in ud-din Chishti, 'Attar & Auhad ud-din Kermani
SELECTED POEMS
Translation & Introduction Paul Smith. Pages 541.

ANTHOLOGY OF WOMEN MYSTICAL POETS
OF THE MIDDLE-EAST & INDIA
Translation & Introduction Paul Smith. Pages 497.

FOUR MORE GREAT CLASSIC SUFI MASTER POETS
Sadi, 'Iraqi, Yunus Emre, Shabistari.
SELECTED POEMS
Translation & Introduction Paul Smith. Pages 562.

~ANOTHER~
FOUR GREAT CLASSIC SUFI MASTER POETS
Amir Khusrau, Ibn Yamin, Hafiz & Nesimi
SELECTED POEMS Translation & Introduction Paul Smith.
Pages 636.

FOUR GREAT LATER CLASSIC SUFI MASTER POETS
Shah Ni'mat'ullah, Jami, Dara Shikoh & Makhfi
···SELECTED POEMS···
Translation & Introduction Paul Smith. Pages 526.

THE FOUR LAST GREAT SUFI MASTER POETS
Shah Latif, Nazir Akbarabadi, Ghalib and Iqbal
···SELECTED POEMS···
Translation & Introduction Paul Smith. Pages 616.

'ATTAR & KHAQANI: SUFI POETRY ~A Daybook~
Translation & Introduction Paul Smith. 388 pages.

POET-SAINTS OF MAHARASHTRA:
SELECTED POEMS
Translations & Introductions by Paul Smith. Pages 198.

ABHANGS & BHAJANS OF THE GREATEST INDIAN
POET-SAINTS
Translations & Introductions Paul Smith. Pages 214.

A TREASURY OF LESSER-KNOWN GREAT SUFI POETS
Translation & Introduction Paul Smith. Pages 736.

HATEF OF ISFAHAN AND HIS FAMOUS TARJI-BAND
Translation & Introduction Paul Smith. Pages 129.

CLASSIC BATTLE POEMS OF ANCIENT INDIA
& ARABIA, PERSIA & AFGHANISTAN
Translation & Introduction Paul Smith. Pages 246.

~ANOTHER~ FIVE GREAT CLASSIC SUFI MASTER
POETS Ibn al-Farid, Ibn 'Arabi, Baba Farid, Baba Afzal, Rumi.
SELECTED POEMS
Translation & Introduction Paul Smith. Pages 626.

ANTHOLOGY OF GREAT SUFI & MYSTICAL POETS
OF PAKISTAN
Translation & Introduction by Paul Smith. Pages 260.

ZARATHUSHTRA: SELECTED POEMS
A New Verse Translation and Introduction by Paul Smith
from the Original Translation by D.J. Irani.
Original Introduction by Rabindranath Tagore. 141 pages.

THE DHAMMAPADA: The Gospel of the Buddha
Revised Version by Paul Smith
from translation from the Pali of F. Max Muller. 247 pages

THE YOGA SUTRAS OF PATANJALI
"The Book of the Spiritual Man" An Interpretation By Charles
Johnston, General Introduction by Paul Smith. Pages 173.

BHAGAVAD GITA: The Gospel of the Lord Shri Krishna
Translated from Sanskrit with Introduction by Shri Purohit Swami,
General Introductions by Charles Johnston, Revised into Modern
English with an Introduction by Paul Smith. 326 pages.

~TAO TE CHING~ by Lao Tzu
Modern English Version by Paul Smith
from the Translation from the Chinese by Paul Carus. Pages 147.

THE PERSIAN ORACLE: Hafiz of Shiraz
Translation, Introduction & Interpretations by Paul Smith
Pages 441.

CAT & MOUSE: Obeyd Zakani
Translation & Introduction by Paul Smith
Large Format, 7" x 10" Illustrated 183 pages

HAFEZ: THE DIVAN
Volume One: The Poems
Revised Translation Paul Smith "7 x 10" 578 pages

HAFEZ: THE DIVAN
Volume Two: Introduction
Paul Smith 7" x 10" 224 pages.

~ SAADI ~ THE DIVAN
Revised Translation & Introduction Paul Smith
7" x 10" 548 pages.

HAFEZ: BOOK OF DIVINATION
Translation, Introduction & Interpretations by Paul Smith
Large Format Edition, 7" x 10" 441 pages

LAYLA AND MAJNUN: NIZAMI
Translation & Introduction by Paul Smith
Large Format Edition, 7" x 10" 239 pages.

HAFEZ: DIVAN
Revised Translation, Introduction Etc by Paul Smith
Large Format Edition 7" x 10" 800 pages.

HAFEZ OF SHIRAZ:
The Life, Poetry and Times of the Immortal Persian Poet
Books 1.2 & 3. (The Early Years, The Middle Years, The Later
Years) by Paul Smith
Large Format Edition 7" x 10" over 800 pages each book.

OMAR KHAYYAM: RUBA'IYAT
Translation & Introduction Paul Smith
Reprint of 1909 Introduction by R.A. Nicholson
Large Format Edition, 7" x 10" Illustrated, 280 pages.

ROSE GARDEN OF MYSTERY: SHABISTARI
Translation by Paul Smith.
Introduction by E.H. Whinfield & Paul Smith
Large Format Edition 7" x 10" 182 pages.

SUFIS, PRINCESSES & DERVISHES, MARTYRS &
FEMINISTS: Ten Great Women Poets of the East
Translations & Introductions Paul Smith
Large Format Edition 7" x 10" 410 pages.

ARABIC SUFI POETRY: An Anthology
Translation & Introduction Paul Smith
Large Format Edition 7" x 10" 387 pages.

A QUILT OF WOMEN SPIRITUAL POETS OF THE
MIDDLE-EAST & INDIA
Translation & Introduction Paul Smith
Large Format Edition 7" x 10" 509 pages.

THE BOOK OF ABU SA'ID
Ruba'iyat... Life & Times & Teachings
Translation by Paul Smith
Large Format Edition 7" x 10" 350 pages.

THE BOOK OF KABIR
Short Poems *(Sakhis)*
Translation & Introduction Paul Smith
Large Format Edition 7" x 10" 698 pages.

~RUMI~ *Ruba'iyat*
Translation & Introduction Paul Smith
Large Format Edition 7" x 10" 368 pages

THE BOOK OF FARID AL-DIN 'ATTAR
Ruba'is, Ghazals & Masnavis
Translation & Introduction Paul Smith
Large Format Edition 7" x 10" 207 pages

THE BOOK OF OBEYD ZAKANI
Poetry, Prose, Satire, Jokes and Ribaldry.
Translation and Introduction by Paul Smith
Large Format Edition 7" x 10" 357 pages.

THE BOOK OF MANSUR HALLAJ
Selected Poems & The Tawasin
Translation & Introduction Paul Smith
Large Format Edition 7" x 10" 323 pages

THE BOOK OF RUMI
Ruba'is, Ghazals, Masnavis and a *Qasida*
Translation & Introduction Paul Smith
Large Format Edition 7" x 10" 476 pages.

THE BOOK OF SARMAD
Translation & Introduction Paul Smith
Large Format Edition 7" x 10" 407 pages

THE BOOK OF IBN AL-FARID
Translation & Introduction Paul Smith
Large Format Edition 7" x 10" 178 pages

THREE SUFI-MARTYR POETS OF INDIA
Sarmad, Dara Shikoh & Makhfi
Translation & Introduction Paul Smith
Large Format Edition 7" x 10" pages 334.

THE BOOK OF KHAQANI
Translation & Introduction by Paul Smith
Large Format Paperback 7' x 10" pages 230

DRUNK ON GOD
Anthology Poems by God-Realized & God-Intoxicated Poets
Translation & Introduction by Paul Smith
Large Format Paperback 7" x 10" pages 804.

POETRY OF INDIA
Anthology of the Greatest Poets of India
Translations, Introductions by Paul Smith
Large Format 7" x 10" Pages 760

THE BOOK OF JAMI
Translation & Introduction by Paul Smith
Large Format Paperback 7" x 10" pages 233.

THE BOOK OF ANSARI
Translation & Introduction by Paul Smith
Large Format Paperback 7" x 10" pages 231.

YUNUS EMRE & NESIMI:
THE TWO GREAT TURKISH SUFI POETS...
Their Lives & a Selection of their Poems
Translation & Introduction Paul Smith
Large Format Paperback 7" x 10" 416 pages.

THE BOOK OF NESIMI
Translation & Introduction by Paul Smith
Large Format Paperback 7" x 10" pages 250.

THE BOOK OF IQBAL
Translation & Introduction by Paul Smith
Large Format Paperback 7" x 10" pages 252.

THE BOOK OF 'IRAQI
Translation & Introduction by Paul Smith
Large Format Paperback 7" x 10" pages 186.

THE BOOK OF TURKISH POETRY
Anthology of Sufi, Dervish, Divan, Court & Folk Poetry
from the 12th – 20th Century
Translation & Introduction Paul Smith
7" x 10" Large Format Paperback 341 pages

THE BOOK OF HAFIZ (HAFEZ)
Translation, Introduction Etc. Paul Smith
Large Format Edition 7" x 10" 532 pages.

THE BOOK OF SANA'I
Translation & Introduction Paul Smith
Large Format Paperback 167 pages.

THE BOOK OF ECSTASY OR
THE BALL & THE POLO-STICK
by 'Arifi
Translation & Introduction Paul Smith
Large Format Paperback 7" x 10" 221 pages.

ANTHOLOGY OF SUFI & FOLK STROPHE POEMS
OF PERSIA AND THE INDIAN SUB-CONTINENT
Translation & Introduction Paul Smith
Large Format Paperback 7" x 10" 423 pages.

~Introduction to Sufi Poets Series~

Life & Poems of the following Sufi poets, Translations &
Introductions: Paul Smith

'AISHAH AI-BA'UNIYAH, AMIR KHUSRAU, ANSARI, ANVARI, AL-MA'ARRI, 'ATTAR, ABU SA'ID, AUHAD UD-DIN, BABA FARID, BABA AZFAL, BABA TAHIR, BEDIL, BULLEH SHAH, DARA SHIKOH, GHALIB, HAFIZ, IBN 'ARABI, IBN YAMIN, IBN AL-FARID, IQBAL, INAYAT KHAN, 'IRAQI, JAHAN KHATUN, JAMI, KAMAL AD-DIN, KABIR, KHAQANI, KHAYYAM, LALLA DED, MAKHFI, MANSUR HALLAJ, MU'IN UD-DIN CHISHTI, NAZIR AKBARABADI, NESIMI, NIZAMI, OBEYD ZAKANI, RAHMAN BABA, RUMI, SANA'I, SADI, SARMAD, SHABISTARI, SHAH LATIF, SHAH NI'MAT'ULLAH, SULTAN BAHU, YUNUS EMRE, EARLY ARABIC SUFI POETS, EARLY PERSIAN SUFI POETS, URDU SUFI POETS, TURKISH SUFI POETS, AFGHAN SUFI POETS 90 pages each.

POETRY

THE MASTER, THE MUSE & THE POET
An Autobiography in Poetry
by Paul Smith. 654 Pages.

~A BIRD IN HIS HAND~
POEMS FOR AVATAR MEHER BABA
by Paul Smith. 424 pages.

PUNE: THE CITY OF GOD (A Spiritual Guidebook to the New Bethlehem)
Poems & Photographs in Praise of Avatar Meher Baba
by Paul Smith. 159 pages.

COMPASSIONATE ROSE
Recent *Ghazals* for Avatar Meher Baba
by Paul Smith. 88 pages.

~THE ULTIMATE PIRATE~
(and the Shanghai of Imagination)
A FABLE by Paul Smith. 157 pages.

+THE CROSS OF GOD+
A Poem in the *Masnavi* Form
by Paul Smith (7 x 10 inches)

RUBA'IYAT ~ of ~ PAUL SMITH
Pages 236.

SONG OF SHINING WONDER
& OTHER *MASNAVI* POEMS
Paul Smith. Pages 171.

~TEAMAKER'S *DIVAN... GHAZALS*~
Paul Smith. Pages 390.

CRADLE MOUNTAIN
Paul Smith... Illustrations – John Adam.
(7x10 inches) Second Edition.

~BELOVED & LOVER~
Ghazals by Paul Smith... inspired by Meher Baba
Pages 410.

POEMS INSPIRED BY 'GOD SPEAKS' BY MEHER BABA
Paul Smith... Pages 168.

MEHER BABA'S SECLUSION HILL
Poems & Photographs by Paul Smith "7 x 10" 120 pages.

FICTION

THE FIRST MYSTERY A Novel of the Road...
by Paul Smith. 541 pages. Large Format Edition 589 pages

~THE HEALER AND THE EMPEROR~
A Historical Novel Based on a True Story
by Paul Smith Pages 149.

>>>GOING<<<BACK...
A Novel by Paul Smith. 164 pages.

THE GREATEST GAME
A Romantic Comedy Adventure With A Kick!
by Paul Smith 187 pages.

- GOLF IS MURDER! A Miles Driver Golfing Mystery
by Paul Smith. 176 pages.

THE ZEN-GOLF MURDER!
A Miles Driver Golfing Mystery
by Paul Smith 146 pages.

~RIANA~ A Novel
by Paul Smith 154 pages.

CHILDREN'S FICTION

PAN OF THE NEVER-NEVER
by Paul Smith 167 pages.

~HAFIZ~
The Ugly Little Boy who became a Great Poet
by Paul Smith 195 pages.

SCREENPLAYS

>>>GOING<<<BACK...
A Movie of War & Peace Based on a True Story ...
Screenplay by Paul Smith

HAFIZ OF SHIRAZ
The Life, Poetry and Times of the Immortal Persian Poet.
A Screenplay by Paul Smith

LAYLA & MAJNUN BY NIZAMI
A Screenplay by Paul Smith

PAN OF THE NEVER-NEVER...
A Screenplay by Paul Smith

THE GREATEST GAME
A Romantic Comedy Adventure With A Kick!
A Screenplay
by Paul Smith

GOLF IS MURDER!
Screenplay
by Paul Smith

THE HEALER & THE EMPEROR
A True Story... Screenplay
by Paul Smith

THE * KISS ... A Screen-Play
by Paul Smith

THE ZEN-GOLF MURDER!
A Screenplay by Paul Smith

TELEVISION

HAFIZ OF SHIRAZ:
A Television Series
by Paul Smith

THE FIRST MYSTERY
A Television Series For The New Humanity
by Paul Smith

THE MARK: The Australian Game
A Thirteen-Part Doco-Drama for Television
by Paul Smith

PLAYS, MUSICALS

HAFIZ: THE MUSICAL DRAMA by Paul Smith

THE SINGER OF SHIRAZ
A Radio Musical-Drama on the Life of Persia's Immortal Poet,
Hafiz of Shiraz by Paul Smith

ART

MY DOGS
From the Sketchbooks of Gus Cohen.   8" x 10" 224 pages

A BRIDGE TO THE MASTER ... MEHER BABA
Paintings & Drawings, Poems & Essays
by Oswald Hall
Edited & Introduction by Paul Smith   8" x 10" 337 pages.

MY VIEW
From the Sketchbooks of Gus Cohen,
Barkers Creek Castlemaine 8" x 10" 210 pages.

THE ART OF KEVIN SMITH
Paintings & Drawings, Sculpture, Furniture,
Mirrors, Boxes & Photographs
8" x 10" 337 pages full colour

> "To penetrate into the essence of all being and significance
> and to release the fragrance of that inner attainment
> for the guidance and benefit of others, by expressing
> in the world of forms, truth, love, purity and beauty...
> this is the only game which has any intrinsic and absolute
> worth. All other, happenings, incidents and attainments can,
> in themselves, have no lasting importance."
> Meher Baba

Made in the USA
San Bernardino, CA
09 December 2017